CW00381618

# Sarum Chronicle

## recent historical research on Salisbury & district

Issue 15: 2015

ISBN 978-0-9571692-6-5        ISSN: 1475-1844

How to contact us:
To order a copy phone Ruth Newman on 01722 328922 or email ruth. tanglewood@btinternet.com

For other titles in the *Sarum Studies* series and for back issues of *Sarum Chronicle* please contact Jane Howells on 01722 331426 or email as below.

To submit material for consideration in future editions of *Sarum Chronicle* email Jane Howells at jane@sarum-editorial.co.uk with the words Sarum Chronicle in the subject line.

Editorial Team: Roy Bexon, John Chandler, Chris Clark, John Cox, Kate Crouch, John Elliott, Jane Howells, Andrew Minting, Ruth Newman, Margaret Smith

www.sarumchronicle.wordpress.com

Designed and typeset by John Elliott

# Contents

# Editorial

*Sarum Chronicle* enters its fifteenth edition in good heart and there continues to be no risk that we might run out of subjects on Salisbury and the surrounding area.

This year we have returned to our eclectic mix of articles. We are always particularly pleased to welcome new authors with such a surprising range of topics; from the history of the veterinary surgeons of Salisbury, to Milford ice houses, the Salisbury-Saintes twinning and a delightful account of a 19th century resident in the College of Matrons. At the same time we are exceedingly grateful to our familiar contributors, including two past members of the editorial board, who continue to use *Sarum Chronicle* to publish their wide ranging research.

The *Sarum Chronicle* annual lecture proved a sell out last November and we were not disappointed. In a topical and superbly delivered lecture, Dr Alan Crosby gave a brilliant summary of the vicissitudes of King John, which is reproduced in this issue.

During 2014 we published a new volume in our Sarum Studies series, *Women in Salisbury Cathedral Close*, the first study of women from the 13th to the 21st centuries, who were connected with the Close. This has proved popular, and apt in the year when women were granted full equality within the church.

A few of the editorial board have been with the *Chronicle* since its inception and have seen it develop and establish itself as a regular part of Salisbury's history scene. We are all busy volunteers and so new committee members are much appreciated. John Cox, retired Head of English at Bishop Wordsworth's School, has provided valuable literary skills whilst Roy Bexon has already proved a tower of strength with his photographic expertise, smoothing over the angst of preparing illustrations for final publication. Kate Crouch and Chris Clark have helped to ensure that the administration runs efficiently behind the scenes.

As ever we rely on your continued support to guarantee our future existence.

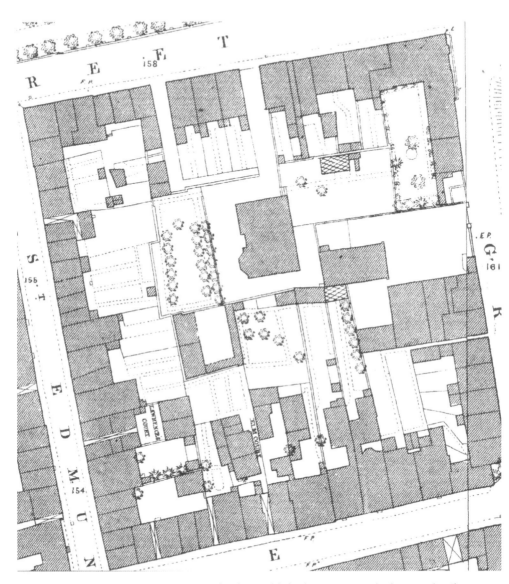

Fig 1: Ordnance Survey 1:500 scale plan, published 1880, Vanner's chequer detail

# Vanner's Chequer: new light on a corner of Medieval Salisbury, part 1

## John Chandler

During June and July 2013 Wessex Archaeology on behalf of Bargate Homes Ltd undertook archaeological investigation in advance of proposed housing development across the centre of Vanner's chequer from Bedwin Street to Salt Lane.[1] This was the first time that the chequer[2] had been the subject of archaeological excavation and the purpose of this paper, ahead of publication of the full report, is to consider from the documentary sources available the early history and development of this corner of Salisbury, in the light of these recent archaeological discoveries. A second part, to be completed later, will look at the chequer's more recent history.

Vanner's chequer, at the north-eastern corner of the medieval grid, and furthest from the market place, is almost square, 80m x 87m, which equates to approximately 16 x 17.5 perches (Fig 1).[3] Unlike its narrower neighbour to the south, Griffin chequer (14 perches wide), it cannot, therefore, be regularly divided into medieval Salisbury's standard tenement size, of 7 x 3 perches. Its slightly enlarged width is probably because it seems to have lain open on its eastern side to the Greencroft, and was not built up along this frontage until the 18th century.[4] Although it was somewhat peripheral to the city's commercial heart it had an important neighbour in St Edmund's collegiate church to its north, as well as the citizens' open space, the Greencroft, to the east.

Several of Salisbury's chequers did not acquire their present names until the 17th century. Richard Vanner (or Vannard) occupied a tenement in the chequer in 1651, and this is the earliest reference to the name.[5] He was warden of the Salisbury tailors' company in 1669, but little else is known about him.[6] In 1625 the chequer may have been referred to by the name of another occupant, Henry Greeneway, since 'Greenawaye's Chequer', so-called, included among its poor residents the family of John Kengington, who was leasing a tenement in what was to became Vanner's chequer from 1619.[7] A tax assessment of 1657 describes it as Mr John Fishlock's chequer (Fishlock was Vanner's landlord).[8] Evidence for its medieval name is offered below but, as this must remain a little speculative, it will be best to consider first the 17th century.

Abundant documentation among the city records relates to the properties lining the western (St Edmund's Church Street) and northern (now Bedwin Street) frontages of the chequer, at least from about 1590 onwards, since most were, or had been for a time, the property of the mayor and commonalty, as Salisbury's government was known.[9] The names of successive lessees, the extent of their tenements, and in some cases Victorian plans of their buildings, are all preserved. From these details it is possible to construct part of a somewhat unusual jigsaw puzzle (Fig 2), of which all the pieces are rectangles, but many of them are missing – including those that would relate to the parts of the chequer excavated in 2013. In mitigation the surviving leases often describe the abuttals – the properties that they adjoin – and there are various other sources to help us.

Along the St Edmund's Church Street frontage running northwards from Salt Lane, the first six tenements, as recorded between the 1590s and 1716, were of similar dimensions, equating to four perches deep and one-and-one-third wide. This consistency may once have continued to the Bedwin Street corner, as the 'four-perch' boundary line still divided some of the properties in the north of the chequer in 1880. For most of its length it is reflected in the western boundary of the recent housing development (and the limit, therefore, of archaeological investigations). From this period nos 68 and 70 St Edmund's Church Street have retained roof timbers and some timber framing,[10] and they are probably the two cottages leased to William Grafton in 1594,[11] one of which was later tenanted by the Kengington family; their employment in quilling and spinning was overseen in 1625 by the officials charged with setting the poor to work.[12] The subsequent history of this pair of cottages, including two Victorian plans (Fig 3), is chronicled in the city archives up to 1877, when following an auction they were acquired by Henry Neesham, cutler, of Oatmeal Row.[13]

Land in the centre of the chequer, immediately to the east of the 'four-perch' line, did not belong to the mayor and commonalty, but to two private owners, and successive ownership can be deduced from the abuttals referred to above. The dividing line between the two properties was a wall, part of

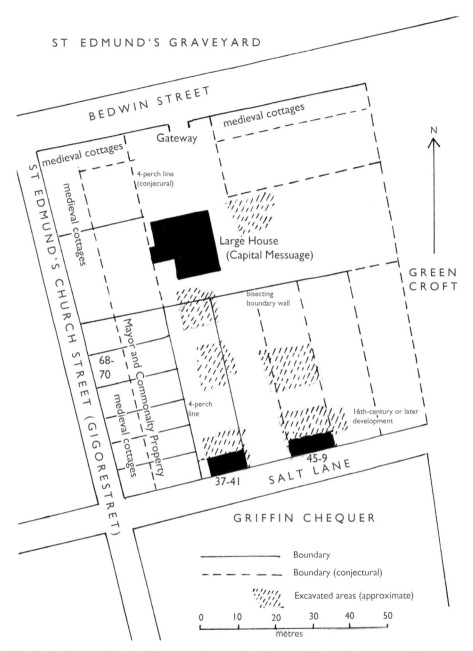

Fig 2: Conjectural plan of Vanner's chequer, showing possible early layout and features discussed in the text

which was excavated in 2013, and found to have been originally built of chalk and flint rubble 0.4m thick, but later patched up and repaired, and

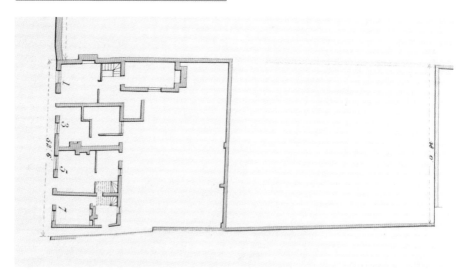

Fig 3: Detail from plan by J M Peniston of cottages in St Edmund's Church Street, 1859 (WSA G23/701/31, plan 12)

eventually rebuilt in brick. It appears to have bisected the chequer (apart from the tenements along the western frontage) into two equal halves, since its distance from Bedwin Street and Salt Lane is the same. South of this wall was a stone-lined medieval shaft, interpreted as a cess pit, and a number of rubbish pits of various dates. They presumably lay at the far end of a garden or backland which extended northwards from a substantial medieval house fronting Salt Lane (on the site of nos 37–41), which was also excavated in 2013.

Three phases in the development of this site were identified. The earliest, comprising pits, postholes and stakeholes forming no coherent pattern, was replaced by a substantial chalk and stone built house, probably during the 13th or 14th century. It seems to have comprised a large rectangular hall, parallel with Salt Lane, and was refurbished in the 15th or 16th century, with internal divisions, walls of flint and greensand, and new floor layers. The house was later rebuilt, using brick, and adding substantial outbuildings to the rear.

The medieval owners of this house have not been traced. The first name we can pin to it from the abuttals is that of George Wilton, who paid pew rent at St Edmund's church in 1551, entertained a travelling singer in 1568/9 and died about 1570, leaving a legacy to his church.[14] During the 1590s and in 1601 it belonged to William Burnett, who also had paid pew rent, in 1587/8, and who was described as a victualler when he died in 1612.[15] An inventory was made of his possessions, described room-by-room, and this may well relate to the excavated house in Salt Lane. His house had a hall, buttery and parlour on the ground floor, with three chambers above and a 'back house', stable and yard. He was not a particularly wealthy man, and his most valuable possession was linen, kept in chests in the parlour, suggesting that linen-draper may have been a more accurate description of his livelihood.

After Burnett George Paige was probably the next owner, recorded in 1618, but when he died in 1631, described as a grocer, he was living in St Thomas's parish.[16] The next name we have is Thomas Barwick, who was the non-resident owner with one tenant in 1651 and two in 1667, but he had gone by 1687.[17] Then there is a disappointing silence until 1716, when a Mr Sibly, presumably Joseph Sibly, a clothier who died in 1742, was in possession. The next recorded owner, before 1780, was Joseph Warne,[18] described as a gentleman c1795.[19]

Along the southern frontage of the chequer, little has been discovered of the early owners of the properties which lay east of the excavated house (37–41 Salt Lane). The archaeological work in 2013 included investigating the site of 45–9 Salt Lane, three cottages which had survived long enough, before demolition c1967 or later, to have been surveyed and described by the Royal Commission.[20] They had timber-framed walls with brick facing and tiled roofs, and probably dated from the 16th century. The excavations suggested that before they were built there had not previously been houses on the site, and that what became their backlands had been used as medieval rubbish pits and for quarrying. The surviving tax lists of the period 1651–1704 include several names of owners or tenants who cannot be located elsewhere in the chequer, so it is likely that they held land and houses in this area.[21] But so far no topographical sequence can be identified in the lists.

The interior of the chequer, north of the dividing east–west wall, was and is dominated by a house used until the recent redevelopment as Salisbury register office. This building, and those to its north fronting Bedwin Street, have been retained, so no archaeological investigation was possible in this area. This substantial house, however, dates only from the later 19th century. A large-scale plan of Salisbury (Fig 4), made in 1854,[22] plots instead a house of similar size, whose footprint lay mostly to the west of it. It appears to have faced north, looking towards St Edmund's church, and was approached from Bedwin Street by a large forecourt or driveway area, similar to, but smaller than, that of the College (Bourne Hill) nearby, which was flanked by trees or shrubs, and with a circular clump of greenery in its centre. A substantial building, in a similar position, is also shown on the much less accurate Salisbury plan of 1716.[23]

Fig 4: Composite plan derived from sheets of a drainage map of Salisbury, 1854, showing Vanner's Chequer (WSA, G23/701/1PC, plans 9, 10, 13)

No evidence for the age or appearance of this house has been found,[24] but the abuttals tell us who owned the site in the 1580s (Thomas Grafton), 1593 (William Holcrafte), 1618 (John Banger), and 1716 (Jeffery Everatt). Grafton served as St Edmund's churchwarden in 1584/5,[25] and Holcrafte was also lessee of the Greencroft from 1602,[26] when he was described as a gentleman. John Banger was Salisbury's mayor in 1638.[27] Jeffery Everatt, when he died c1720, owned not only this principal house, but also four others in Salt Lane and three more in St Edmund's Church Street.[28] Four other men can be associated with the house during the intervening period, since they were by far the largest taxpayers in the chequer. These were Mr Reade in 1651,[29] John Fishlake between 1657 and 1670,[30] Robert Grayly in 1699 and Samuel Fishlake in 1704.[31] John Fishlake was perhaps the father of another John, who served as rector of Fisherton Anger, 1693–1731.[32]

All the evidence discovered from the Elizabethan period onwards, therefore, suggests that, concealed from the street by a regular row of cottages to the west, and perhaps another to the north, a large and highly-rated house with a sequence of locally distinguished owners existed in the northern half of the chequer. An entry in the 1618 survey, which refers to cottages facing St Edmund's graveyard, next to John Banger's gate and with his property behind,[33] implies that this house stood back from the street, so it may be reasonable to equate it with the building depicted in 1716 and 1854. Furthermore, it is possible to trace its history back into the medieval period. In 1455 Thomas Freeman, a wealthy mercer and alderman with a reputation for causing trouble both before and during his year as mayor in 1436/7,[34] was taxed on a number of properties, including a messuage (a house with outbuildings and land) opposite St Edmund's graveyard which had formerly belonged to John Lake, and a garden opposite the graveyard which had been John Cheney's.[35] The assessment for this messuage, 23d, was far higher than for most properties, which was typically between 3d and 11d.

Thomas Freeman's house must have remained a family property after his death, because in 1504 Richard Freeman in his will bequeathed it to his grandson, John Redberd.[36] The will includes several details which illuminate the topography of the area at the time. As well as the 'capitall messuage', there is another house with a tenant, Henry Borrage, nearby; there is a stone house 'afore the college [i.e. the collegiate church] of St Edmunds with the barn thereby and with all the tenements set and lying between the said stone house and the gate of my capital place'; and there is another house with two tenements between it and the gate. But Redberd, who must have been a minor at the time of his grandfather's death, seems not to have enjoyed his inheritance. His trustees had somehow parted with the deeds, and the family twice brought the case to chancery to try to retrieve them, firstly in 1515 or earlier, and then between 1518 and 1529.[37] In the latter case Redberd's son, Richard, accused one Simon Gilford of refusing to give them up. Whether or not he was successful is unknown, and the trail goes cold until Thomas Grafton in the 1580s.

Reverting to Thomas Freeman in 1455, his entries in the tax list offer further clues about his surroundings. In addition to the messuage and garden described above, and sandwiched between them in the list, is a cottage and tenement in 'Nuggeston', lately of Stephen Harte, and two tenements on the corner of 'Nuggeston'. In itself this juxtaposition need not be significant, as the tax list is arranged by owner rather than location. But Nuggeston occurs sporadically in deeds and lists beginning in the first century of Salisbury's existence and, when identifiable, always in connection with this corner of

Salisbury. A deed of 1340 concerns a tenement in 'Gigorestret' (the name then applied to the whole line, including Pennyfarthing Street and St Edmund's Church Street), and is endorsed, in Latin, 'two cottages next to the corner in Nhuggeston'.[38] A rent roll from as late as 1565 includes a heading 'Nuggestonestret alias St Edmundstrete', followed by 20 names, including William Grafton – whom we have encountered there 30 years later, and perhaps a kinsman of Thomas, who owned the big house.[39] Confusingly, a deed of 1571 describes a cottage on the south side of Salt Lane as 'in a street called Nuggeston Street alias Salt Lane leading to a green crofte alias Greencrofte'.[40] A list of rents from mayor and commonalty property in 1412/13 includes a corner shop or cottage in Nuggeston towards St Edmund's church, and this is followed by another six cottages there, the last one described as next to John Lake's cottage.[41] John Lake's tenement, it will be recalled, when in 1455 it belonged to Thomas Freeman, was described as standing opposite St Edmund's graveyard. Thus the curious name Nuggeston was applied at various times to three of the streets which surround Vanner's chequer, and the inference to be drawn is that it was used for the chequer itself, or – a little more cautiously – for tenements in the north-eastern quarter of the city.

There is rather more to be said of these cottages which lined what is now called Bedwin Street opposite St Edmund's church, and along St Edmund's Church Street, the northern and western frontages of Vanner's chequer. Two characteristics of the latter, their regularity and their ownership by the mayor and commonalty, have been noted, and these are shared also by those along the northern frontage. Not until 1406 was the city permitted to acquire property as a corporate body in mortmain (perpetuity), and there followed a flurry of acquisitions, including cottages which were then let to tenants.[42] In 1409, for instance, John Teynterer bequeathed to the city six cottages which he owned in Nuggeston;[43] Richard Pynnock likewise, the following year, left the city an inn and three houses.[44] Before 1413 John Baker, a Salisbury grocer, had sold the city a group of cottages in 'Nhuggeston towards St Edmund's Church' which in 1419 were then let to John Parch for 20 years on a repairing lease.[45] These cottages seem to have involved the city in a legal dispute with one John Kingsbridge which involved taking the title deeds to London,[46] and they may be the six cottages sold with other city properties in 1445 in order to fund repairs to dilapidated houses.[47] By 1455 John Parch had only one house left in Nuggeston, but had invested in four tenements in Rolveston nearby.[48]

Nuggeston and Rolveston are unusual names in an urban context, and unlike any others from medieval Salisbury. Rolveston, from which the surviving Rollestone Street derives, was supposedly named from one Rolf who built houses there;[49] and it is reasonable to suppose that Nuggeston originated in the same way – so we are to infer the meaning 'Rolf's estate', 'Nhug's estate'.[50] Hugh Nhug (the 'h' usually intrudes in variants of the name) was living in a house on the corner of Blue Boar Row and Endless Street in 1268,[51] which was therefore known as Nuggescorner.[52] Hugh le Nhug was a juror in an inquiry held at Salisbury in 1299 over houses acquired in the city by Amesbury priory,[53] and he and John le Nhugg were among the citizens who ratified an agreement with the bishop in 1306 following a dispute over a tax called tallage in 1302.[54] In his will,[55] made in 1332, John left to his wife the house they lived in with two adjoining shops (perhaps Nuggescorner),[56] but also four adjoining shops next to a house called 'Brewerne' (brewhouse),[57] a house occupied by John atte Barre, and one other house. His wish was that after Edith's death most of this property would be sold. This is probably what happened, because in the same bundle of deeds is a grant to Andrew of Langford from his mother, dated 1351, of six cottages and a grange in Nuggeston, and his will of 1357 by which he returned them all to her. Another deed in the bundle may also reflect the dispersal of the Nhug estate, since it describes a house in Nuggeston in 1363 which a widow bequeathed to the city but (this being before the city could hold property) the mayor very correctly sold it.

The last Nhugg recorded as resident in Salisbury was perhaps Philip le Nuygh, who in 1340 lived in 'Gigorestret' next to a corner in Nuggeston.[58] He may have been the brother of the John le Nhugg who left the will, because they are mentioned together in one more deed, which seems to take us right back to the founding of the city. In 1348 the daughter of one Stephen Glendy of Stratford sub Castle forfeited her interest in the rent from property which her father had sold to John and Philip, and to William Sauntel.[59] It is described as 'certain sites or tenements lying in . . . Martinescroft in the streets called Chiperstret and Brounstret'. The intersection of these streets lies west of Vanner's chequer, but the deed seems to be harking back to a period before the Rolfs and the Nhugs, or even earlier speculators, had been developing the northern chequers, when the area was still farmland within the parish of St Martin's.[60] If this is correct, today's Greencroft may be seen as a surviving relic of this larger 'Martinescroft'.

To recapitulate, a plausible reconstruction of the creation of Vanner's chequer might be that it was developed on its western and northern sides soon after the city's grid of streets was laid out across farmland ('Martin's Croft') during the 13th century. Instrumental in the building of cottages with small tenements in this and the neighbouring area were the families of Rolf and Nhug, from which they took their names. There was also a brewhouse in the vicinity. Vanner's chequer, as it would be named in the 17th century, was bisected into northern and southern halves by a significant wall, to the north of which a large house existed by *c*1400, approached by a gateway opposite St Edmund's church. Houses were also built along the chequer's southern edge, Salt Lane, but probably not as far as its south-eastern corner until the end of the middle ages. After 1400 the mayor and commonalty were able to buy and sell cottages in St Edmund's Church Street and Bedwin Street, and still retained a uniform group and several others after 1600, in some cases until the 19th century. Documentation after 1700 is prolific, and the modern history of the chequer will be the subject of a second paper, planned for the next issue of *Sarum Chronicle*.[61]

## Notes

1. The excavation was directed by Phil Harding, to whom I am greatly indebted for information and advice. This and an adjacent excavation are to be published as: P Harding, 'Excavations in Vanner's and Griffin Chequers, Salisbury: A study of urban development' *WANHM*, forthcoming.
2. 'Chequers' in Salisbury are the quadrilateral blocks of land defined by the medieval gridded street plan.
3. Based on OS 1:500 mapping (see Fig 1). A perch was 16ft 6in, approximately 5m.
4. There were no houses there in 1751 or 1753: W Naish, *Map of Salisbury* (1751 ed); WSA, G23/1/272.
5. WSA, G23/1/176.
6. C Haskins, *Ancient trade guilds and companies of Salisbury* (1912), 217-18. A Newbury apothecary of the same name appears to have had interests in Salisbury and Shaftesbury in 1654: TNA, C 6/129/215.
7. For 1625 list, P A Slack (ed) *Poverty in early Stuart Salisbury* (1975), 69; for Greeneway and Kengington: WSA, G23/1/68, ff 40, 45 (1st pagination).
8. WSA, G23/1/177, f 13.
9. Most evidence presented in this and the next paragraph is derived from WSA, G23/1/68; G23/1/69.
10. RCHM, *Salisbury* I (1980), 146 (no 411).
11. WSA, G23/1/68, f 45.
12. Slack, *Poverty*, 69.
13. WSA, G23/1/69, f 37; G23/1/70, f 22; G23/701/30, plan 15; G23/701/31, plan 12.
14. H J F Swayne, *Churchwardens' Accounts of S Edmund and S Thomas, Sarum* (1896), 278, 283, 284.
15. *Ibid*, 135, P4/1612/3.
16. WSA, P4/1631/18.
17. WSA, G23/1/177; *WANHM* 36 1910, 431; WSA G23/150/31, deed of 1687 (abuttal).

18 WSA, G23/1/70.

19 K.H. Rogers (ed.) *Early Trade Directories of Wiltshire* (1992), 30.

20 RCHM, *Salisbury* I (1980), 147 (nos. 417–18).

21 One owner was Humphrey Beckham, the celebrated joiner who has a monument in St Thomas's church.

22 WSA, G23/701/1PC plans 9 and 13.

23 W Naish, *Map of Salisbury* (1716 ed), reproduced in RCHM, *Salisbury* I, pl.16.

24 A watercolour by J M W Turner of St Edmund's church *c*1799 (British Museum, TWO 381, Wilton 205) may depict the chimneys and roofline of this building. It is reproduced in Ian Warrell, *Turner's Wessex: Architecture and Ambition* (2015), 59.

25 Swayne, *Churchwarden's Accounts*, 384.

26 WSA, G23/1/68, f 50 (1st pagination).

27 Slack, *Poverty*, 64.

28 WSA, P1/E/183.

29 WSA, G23/1/176.

30 WSA, G23/1/177-80; *WANHM* 36 1910, 430.

31 WSA, G23/1/181; G23/1/188.

32 *Alumni Oxonienses, 1500-1714*, 502. John (senior) was perhaps a maltster from Durnford, who died in Salisbury in 1688: WSA, P5/1688/31.

33 WSA, G23/1/68, typescript copy, p 6.

34 D R Carr (ed) *First General Entry Book of the City of Salisbury* (2001), xxx, 160 (no. 326). He is also spelled Freman.

35 *WANHM* 37 (1911), 82.

36 WSA, G23/150/86.

37 TNA, C 1/132/33; /C 1/560/52. Neither case can be precisely dated.

38 WSA, G23/294/1 (Swayne scrapbook), 38.

39 WSA, G23/1/68, f 45; G23/1/72, 1565 rent roll.

40 WSA, 799/73.

41 Carr, *First General Entry Book,* 55-6, no 126; cf WSA, G23/1/213, f 110, enrolment of 1412, which may refer to the same cottages. A cottage with tentering racks is also recorded next to John Lake's property: WSA, G23/1/213, f 77.

42 *Cal Pat 1405-8*, 183; *WANHM* 39 1916, 227-9.

43 TNA, C 145/322/18, calendared in *Cal Inq Misc* 8, 210-12, no 380, which misreads his name as 'Tenterelles'.

44 *Ibid.*

45 Carr, *First General Entry Book,* 54–5, nos 125-6; 88, no 201; 90, no 205.

46 *Ibid*, 98, no 217; 248, no 462.

47 *Ibid*, 205, no 397.

48 *WANHM* 37 1911, 83.

49 H Hatcher, *Old and New Sarum, or Salisbury* (1843), 93.

50 *VCH Wilts* 6, 83.

51 Hatcher, *Old and New Sarum*, 52. This odd surname may simply be a variant of 'New', as suggested by D A Crowley, *The Wiltshire Tax List of 1332* (1989), 153 (index entry).

52 Described in RCHM, *Salisbury* I (1980), 133, no 341, and more recently restored.

53 E A Fry (ed), *Abstracts of Wiltshire Inquisitiones post Mortem, 1242-1326* (1908), 238.

54 Hatcher, *Old and New Sarum*, 742.

55 WSA, G23/150/82.

56 In 1332 he was taxed in Market ward: Crowley, *Wiltshire Tax List*, 1.

57 WSA, G23/150/82; the abbreviated Latin appears to be *int' quas dom' que d'r [dicitur?] Brewerne computat'*, which could be construed as 'between which [is] the house which it is said is reckoned a brewhouse. *Brewerne* presumably derives from Old English *breow-aern* 'brewhouse': A H Smith *English Place-Name Elements*, I (1956), 49.

58 WSA, G23/294/1.

59 Sal. Cath. Lib. Dean & Chapter deeds, 1/43.

60 This suggestion was first made by K H Rogers, *Historic Towns, I: Salisbury* (1969), 2 and n.15.

61 My sincere thanks are offered to Phil Harding, Steve Hobbs, Peter Saunders, Emily Naish and Helen Taylor for help in preparing this paper, and to Phil Andrews of Wessex Archaeology for commissioning the research which initiated it. I am grateful to the Wiltshire & Swindon History Centre for allowing me to reproduce photographs of maps and documents. I should also like to pay tribute to the scholarship of Ken Rogers, the late David Carr and the late Christopher Elrington, whose work underpins important parts of it.

# 'King John was not a good man': understanding Magna Carta on its 800th anniversary

## Alan G Crosby

## Introduction

This paper, based on the annual Sarum Chronicle lecture given in November 2014, does not consider the Salisbury copy of Magna Carta but instead explores the background to its creation in the summer of 1215, examining why it is now among the most celebrated and revered documents in the world despite the deeply inauspicious circumstances of its birth. That within a few weeks of those events in the damp meadow beside the Thames at Runnymede the charter was apparently destined to be discredited and forgotten is easily overlooked: the document in fact achieved one of the most remarkable come-backs in archival history.

The early 13th century was a notably turbulent period across much of Western Europe, witnessing historical processes and trends of fundamental importance. Among these were a growing awareness of national identities, the first stirrings of 'popular democracy', social and cultural trends such as growing literacy; and new approaches to administration at different levels of government and in the private affairs of major landowners. Some of these points are revisited later, but it is essential to recognise that Magna Carta did not exist in isolation—it was part of a wide-ranging process of change in society.

In thinking why Magna Carta became so symbolic, it is clear that it has constantly been reinvented. Each age has had its own view of what Magna Carta was and what it stood for. Soon after its creation—by the 1240s—it was becoming a cornerstone of English law, quoted and referred to in legal proceedings, and was being seen as (what it never really was except in the most abstract sense), a guarantee of the liberties of the ordinary man. By the late 15th century the practical value of Magna Carta was greatly diminished, superseded by a vastly more complex, sophisticated and evolving structure of legal precedent, judgment and code. In England by then, parliament played a significant, though still junior, role in government. From the earliest recognisable parliament in 1265, under the rebel Simon de Montfort, at least lip service was paid to Magna Carta as a foundation of the peculiar principle that a sovereign should share some power with some of his subjects. That sense of the charter as a weighty weapon for tempering the excesses of monarchical authority naturally loomed large in the 1620s and 1630s, when James I and Charles I sought to rule without parliament and came into direct conflict with it. What were the rights of a sovereign? What was the relationship between the king and the law? Magna Carta became a symbol of the liberty of parliament (and the people) against the tyranny of a sovereign, a process culminating outside Whitehall Palace on 30 January 1649, when Charles stepped forward to face the axeman.

Thus Magna Carta became a weapon in revolution, symbol of a new philosophy which stated that subjects had the power and, more particularly, the justifiable right to depose an oppressive ruler. That idea bore fruit 130 years later on the other side of the Atlantic, when the overthrow of George III (surely one of the mildest and most likeable of tyrants?) in the American Revolution was truly world-changing. The rights enshrined in the document of 1215 were embodied in some of the most powerful clauses of the new US constitution, and the charter has been central to the principle, though scarcely ever the practice, of American democracy to this day. Furthermore, given the link between the American Revolution and those of France in 1789 and Russia in 1917, we can argue that Magna Carta as a revolutionary tract has been influential, albeit very tenuously, in world affairs through to the present, while its role in helping to shape constitutions and forms of government in countries such as Canada, Australia and New Zealand must not be ignored.

In Victorian England Magna Carta was considered to be the *fons et origo* for the emergence of the particular form of parliamentary democracy with which Britain was uniquely blessed. Its 700th anniversary in 1915 could not be celebrated, but its symbolic importance was unquestioned. This perception, though, was replaced as new perspectives were adopted. In every century, the view of Magna Carta has reflected contemporary preoccupations. That means that in our own time its name is linked with concepts such as human rights and civil liberties. What those who, in the late spring of 1215, so hastily framed the chapters of the document would have made of any later perspectives is beyond imagining.

## The road to Runnymede 1: the loss of Normandy

A A Milne famously stated that 'King John was not a good man', and John's sheer nastiness and vicious untrustworthiness has been acknowledged in English history since his own time. It is one of the popularly accepted building blocks of the royal story—and it is evident that apologists for John have had a hard time, even in an era of more rigorous scholarship and more dispassionate analysis. The future king was born on Christmas Eve 1166 at Beaumont Palace, now the location of a lengthy traffic queue on the western side of Oxford city centre, near the Ashmolean Museum. His parents were Henry II of England (who in reality was hardly English at all) and his fiery, tempestuous wife Eleanor of Aquitaine. Their sensational marriage in 1152, just after her divorce from Louis VII of France, had a profound effect on the history of both countries. They had eight children (five sons and three daughters). John was the youngest of the five and could never have expected to inherit the throne or, indeed, very much at all (hence the mocking name 'Lackland', given to him by his elder brothers). But the eldest surviving son Henry, known as 'the Young King' since he was crowned in their father's lifetime, died childless in 1183, six years before Henry II himself. The next son, Richard, became king but died, also without issue, on 6 April 1199 from wounds received at the siege of Chalûs. The third

King John. Detail from Drawings of the Kings of Britain and England to Henry III, Matthew Paris.
©The British Library Board Cotton Claudius D.VI,f.9v

son, Geoffrey, Duke of Brittany, had died in 1186 leaving a son, Arthur, who was only twelve years old on the death of his uncle Richard. John, already in England, was well-placed to take the throne instead of his young nephew. He seized the opportunity, then rushed over to Normandy and on 24 April was solemnly invested as duke in the cathedral at Rouen. Without any significant opposition, he then returned to England and was crowned at Westminster on 25 May.

This reveals a very different John from the devious prevaricator with whom we are more familiar. When the occasion warranted he could be decisive, quick to respond and indeed dynamic. The events of April 1199 were followed by a crucial diplomatic offensive aimed at Philip II of France, John's rival and the superior lord for some of the French borderlands which John had inherited. Given Arthur of Brittany's better dynastic claim it was essential that John should win French support or, more accurately, that Arthur should not have it. On 22 May this diplomatic campaign bore fruit when Philip publicly acknowledged John's title, as Duke of Normandy, to the potentially contentious lands in Maine, Anjou, Touraine and Poitou. Simultaneously, John was working on another grand strategy. Eleven years previously, a young and landless prince, he had married Isabel, daughter of William, Earl of Gloucester. Now, as a monarch who strode the European stage, he needed something better—especially as his wife had failed to produce children. He immediately annulled the marriage to Isabel and on 24 August 1200 married Isabella, daughter and heiress of Aymer de Valence, Count of Angoulême.

This was in one sense a diplomatic coup, for Angoulême was a large and strategically important semi-independent county on the borders of Normandy. By marrying its heiress John would bring its lands into his Duchy of Normandy, that Continental estate which still mattered so much to the kings of England. But ultimately it was this, as much as any other action, that led to Magna Carta, for Isabella had been betrothed to the powerful lord Hugh de Lusignan, a territorial magnate of high status and influence. Hugh appealed for justice to his superior, Philip II, on the grounds that John had stolen his future wife and broken her betrothal contract. John, also Philip's feudal vassal, was summoned to appear in person to answer, but refused. In April 1202 Philip pronounced judgment, ordering the confiscation of John's lands in Normandy and other territories, and recognising instead the homage and fealty of John's nephew, Arthur of Brittany, as Duke of Normandy. The rights and wrongs of the case itself were secondary questions, since Philip saw the perfect opportunity to make maximum trouble for John, and indeed for Arthur, with the prospect of picking over rich spoils.

In July 1202 war broke out in Normandy between John and his Anglo-Norman forces on the one hand, and on the other Philip and Arthur. John again displayed a fearless determination and dynamism, commanding an army which within a month achieved a crushing victory at Mirabeau. Arthur was captured, the French retreated from John's lands, and in April 1203, on John's orders, his nephew was murdered. Having vanquished his foes, John returned triumphantly to England in December 1203. That was a great mistake. As soon as he had gone Philip II resumed the war, attacking Normandy, now without a resident ruler and disrupted by the earlier fighting. French armies swept across the duchy and in June 1204 occupied Rouen, the capital. Normandy was in French hands. John 'Lackland' had lost the ancestral lands, the hugely symbolic (and wealthy) duchy from which his great-great-grandfather, William the Conqueror, had embarked 138 years before. The humiliation was absolute.

## The king's character

Why did this lead inexorably to Magna Carta? The answer lies in a combination of circumstances. The king was disastrously weakened politically by the loss of Normandy and the turbulent events which followed, while the financial cost of this and subsequent military adventures proved ruinous. This weakness tilted the balance of power in England away from the Crown towards mighty subjects. But we need to consider the wider context, going beyond 'simple' politics, and to investigate the king's character in more detail. As the sovereign was in constitutional terms supremely powerful his personality and actions, rational or otherwise, made a material difference. At the same time far-reaching changes were under way in society, affecting the nature of government itself, which had long antecedents and exceeded the influence of individual monarchs.

History has been extremely unkind to John. His contemporary Matthew Paris, the monk at St Albans who was the earliest chronicler of his troubled reign, had no doubt about the king's unredeemed wickedness: 'Foul as it is, hell itself is defiled by the presence of King John', was his utterly damning verdict. We are told that history is written by the victors: in the other great struggle of his life, against the Church, John seemed unequivocally the loser, so the vitriolic hostility shown by monastic chroniclers comes as no surprise. Because their writings formed the basis of much published history until the 20th century, it is equally unsurprising that Victorian historians were no less condemnatory. Furthermore, during the nineteenth century the 'Whig view of history' prevailed—that is, the belief that the history of England was essentially a march towards progress, enlightenment and the creation of the most perfect system of government the world had ever known. Magna Carta, as progenitor of this system, was revered and the king whose powers it apparently constrained was in consequence reviled.

More recently, historians have sought to redress the balance, not necessarily as part of a rehabilitation exercise but in recognition of the fact that history is infinitely more complex than earlier approaches allowed. Stark black and white depictions are rarely identifiable in the ambiguities of the archival sources and their interpretation. It is unquestioned that John's behaviour was deeply shocking to contemporaries. His hand (or even personal participation) in the murder of his nephew, the savagely vindictive retribution wreaked upon individual opponents, and his sexual licence, all seemed outrageous (never mind that, for example, his great-grandfather Henry I had at least 22 illegitimate children ... strong kings did not attract the same condemnation as weak ones). Occasionally John appears not unattractive to modern eyes; he grew to love his wife Isabella of Angoulême, and enjoyed staying in bed with her until mid-day, but that of course was construed not as a cheerfully romantic nature but as self-indulgent laziness. Intriguingly, he had 'a huge appetite for the nuts and bolts of administration' and intervened personally in matters great and small in the administration of the royal household and the exercise of justice. He had a fascination for the technicalities of government which was shared by few of his successors and fewer of his predecessors and, as one Victorian historian suggested, he was 'the ablest and most ruthless of the Angevins'.[1] Another observed his 'curious combination of shrewdness and slackness, of ability and ineptitude'.[2] But overshadowing this strange mixture of energy and sloth, great competence and evident fecklessness, was a paranoid sense of insecurity and his invariably suspicious, wary and secretive nature. His reputation for duplicity and inconsistency, plotting and deviousness, was richly deserved, though in this he was far from unique among medieval monarchs or indeed later politicians.

## The changes in the wider world

Could anybody have coped adequately with the immense pressures of society itself? Looking at the late 12th and early 13th centuries we see England at a turning point, with a precocious sense of identity and individualism. Rapid economic expansion was evident throughout Europe, as two centuries of climatic improvement gave longer growing seasons and more reliable food supplies, reducing mortality and generating population growth. This stimulated a much-increased level of local, national and international trade, accelerating the shift from a subsistence-style economy towards a monetary system and creating a more sophisticated hierarchy of market centres and trading places. This, in turn, made the landowning class richer—they were the owners of those markets and the beneficiaries of the commercialising agricultural economy. But it also facilitated the emergence of an upwardly mobile merchant trading class, whose arrival helped to destabilise social structures. Wealthier lords were more conscious of their potential power and influence, and wanted a greater say in matters of government, but were also jealously guarding their position against upstart rivals.

The later 12th century saw a rapid growth in literacy, and the shaping of a document-based culture. A generation before, purely oral testimony had been fully acceptable and had legal force, but now fell quickly into disfavour as the presumption was made that only a written document had the reliability and permanence needed for a legal system based on custom and precedent. Accompanying this trend was the construction of a more complex, standardised and systematic structure of legal process, increasingly dependent upon central control and royal administration. The Crown, in principle the fount of justice, now also became its bureaucratic focus. Clarity in the law raised questions, among them the relationship of the king to the laws which he promulgated, but it also generated a proliferation of parchment—recording decisions, keeping accounts, and maintaining registers was ever more basic to government, but that meant the appointment of royal officials and the removal of routine matters from the king's purview. Richard I was absent from England for all but six months of his ten-year reign. Royal officials filled the vacuum and entrenched themselves in administration. Magna Carta, one of our first written constitutional documents, was the child of such processes.

Richard's ten years of uninterrupted foreign warfare, followed by the military adventures of John's early reign, were financially ruinous. By 1205 the country was almost bankrupt, and the coffers were exhausted. John's solution was to impose arbitrary and extortionate taxation and to use a wide range of dubious methods of raising money, going against custom and tradition and treading painfully upon the toes of lords and barons. Questions were surely asked. In what circumstances can the king tax us? Do we have any leverage or power of intervention in that process? Is there a *quid pro quo* (which in a later century would lead to the phrase 'no taxation without representation')?

So, in the years after 1200, grievances, grumbles and outright antagonisms grew apace. A more authoritative king (such as his father Henry II or his grandson Edward I) might have dealt with these, by force of personality or by emollient diplomacy. But John was not authoritative and was anything but emollient. Magna Carta embodies answers to a series of fundamental questions, born of those grievances:

1    Was the king above the law and was an alternative position logically possible, as all law and justice stemmed from the king (a debate extensively aired again in 1635–1649)?
2    What, if any, were the king's obligations to his subjects?
3    Had the king to consult and, if so, with whom, over what, and in which circumstances?
4    What were the rights of individual lords, and of the baronial class, and should they have a role in government?
5    Should, or could, a king be obliged to share power and authority?
6    Could a king be held to account?
7    Could a king who failed be deposed or forced to concede some or all of his authority—and if so, to whom, by whom, and in which circumstances?

## Antecedents and precedents

Magna Carta was not without precedent, and at least hints of answers to some of these questions had existed for centuries. England was far ahead the rest of Europe in this regard. The Anglo-Saxon kings, even the most powerful, regularly consulted with the *witangemot* (literally, 'the meeting of the wise'), leading figures from the nobility and the clergy who gathered to give their opinions, consult and on occasion (such as the death of Edward the Confessor in January 1066) to act as the government of the realm. This device, a distant foreshadowing of the House of Lords, did not survive the Conquest, but Henry I (1100) and Stephen (1135) are known to have issued 'coronation charters' setting out the rights and liberties of the English people, and it is believed by some historians that William I (1066), William II (1087) and Henry II (1154) also did so. Such charters were a recognition that kings, while in principle commanding total and universal loyalty, also had obligations to uphold the interests and rights of their subjects—in other words, to conform to a set of values.

The councils held by John's predecessors also represented the concept of consultation and were assemblies before which laws could be promulgated. William I at Gloucester in 1085 publicly commissioned the Domesday Survey (to ensure that it was not perceived as a secret exercise) and the first results were heard in the council at Sarum in the following year. The councils held by Henry II at Clarendon in 1164 and 1166 saw the declaration of the legal codes which were the earliest major attempt to create systematic public law-making. These were occasional events, but both Williams and Henry I held thrice-yearly 'crown-wearings', when they appeared in public gatherings of the nobility and clergy, wore the regalia of state, and consulted with the assembly. So, while Magna Carta was quite unprecedented in its form and style, and in the circumstances in which it was created, some of the principles it enshrined were far from revolutionary. In many ways, indeed, it was a conservative document—those barons, now more English than Norman, hankered after the good old days when their grandfathers and great-grandfathers had been with the king, not against him ... and when the king had upheld their rights, not trampled on them. A rose-tinted view of history is not new.

## The road to Runnymede 2: the aftermath of defeat

Let us return to the events of the early 13th century. Smarting with the humiliation of losing Normandy, John picked a quarrel with the Church. In July 1205 Hubert Walter, the formidable archbishop of Canterbury, died. John, as was the custom of English kings, nominated his successor, choosing his close ally John de Gray, bishop of Norwich. However, the cathedral clergy at Canterbury proposed their own sub-prior, Reginald. After protracted unholy wranglings Pope Innocent III instead consecrated Stephen Langton, an English cleric who had lived for decades in Paris and was a strong supporter of John's bitter enemy Philip II. John rejected Langton, England was placed under papal interdict, and in 1208 the king was personally excommunicated. Untroubled by this though he was, John could not avoid the opprobrium now heaped upon him from all quarters. He sought diversion by campaigning in 1209–1211 in Scotland, Ireland and North Wales, fighting with notable effectiveness and strongly advancing the English cause in all three realms. In certain circumstances John could be a skilled and decisive leader, but unfortunately this rarely guaranteed the security of his own position.

Four years later, recognising the need for a powerful European ally, he dramatically reached an agreement with the papacy. In a world used to sensational changes of political direction (Nixon in China, Martin McGuinness meeting the Queen) this might not seem strange, but it was distinctly unusual for early 13th century diplomacy. John was a modern man—he didn't have any particular principles, he was not a loyal son of the Church, and if short-term self-interest dictated the overturning of a policy or strategy, so be it. Having the pope as his new best friend meant that he could embark on a new military expedition in France. In February 1214 he invaded via Aquitaine (where he was still the duke) and headed northwards, to the borders of Normandy. On 27 July his mixed army of Englishmen, (including his half brother William Longespée), Normans, Gascons and disaffected Frenchmen was routed by the forces of Philip II at Bouvines.

Less than two months later, as the costs and the casualties came home, the first public stirrings of English baronial discontent were felt. Faced with crippling arbitrary taxation and levies, public and diplomatic humiliation, administrative disintegration, and the flouting and disregarding of customary procedures for legal and social transactions, the aristocracy—or one sector of them—were bitterly antagonistic to John. In the spring of 1215 their pent-up anger spilled over into open defiance. Civil war broke out, the king was swiftly brought to heel, and in May 1215 the barons who opposed him, meeting in conclave, drew up a document setting out their demands for the future governance of England and, more especially, the behaviour of the king and his household.

On 15 June John consented to this document beside the Thames at Runnymede. As Tim Tatton Brown has pointed out, the choice of site was charged with political implications. It lay between Windsor and London and was at the exact meeting place of four of the greatest English dioceses— Winchester, Salisbury, London and Lincoln.[3] As in earlier centuries, an open air public ceremony gave legitimacy, but this was a revolutionary act— forcing an anointed sovereign to concede to the demands of his subjects, to constrain his own powers and prerogatives and to admit the principle of power-sharing.

John had been brought to his knees, for several reasons. There was, foremost, the humiliating and expensive defeat in Normandy in 1214, ten years after the no less humiliating loss of the duchy which was his ancestral inheritance—and all the barons were themselves descended from Norman lords within living memory. There had been ten years of ruthless and unremitting money-raising by the king, accompanied by the manipulation, distorting and bypassing of the law to achieve that goal. John had shown a flagrant disregard of customary and traditional procedures, and had imposed 'king's men' on the structures of local administration, disregarding the privileges and power bases of barons and their feudal vassals. And, less tangibly but crucially, there was the sense that the king simply could not be trusted to govern wisely, fairly or rationally.

**The document itself**

Magna Carta was ratified and, seemingly, the king was tamed. The document was a complicated mixture of principle and pragmatism, in some senses mundane but with fine statements of principle. Chapters 39 and 40, in

Salisbury Cathedral's copy of Magna Carta. Reproduced by permission from Salisbury Cathedral.

particular, have been seen as completely redefining the relationship between the people and the law, and are central to what emerged as western-style democracy: 'No man shall be arrested or imprisoned or disseised or outlawed or exiled or in any way victimised ... except by the lawful judgment of his peers or the law of the land' and 'To no-one will we sell, to no-one will we refuse or delay, right or justice'. Other chapters, though, reveal pragmatic attempts to make a theoretical model of how a king should govern into a workable reality. For example, limits were placed on his exercise of feudal rights, and on the reliefs, or cash sums, which he could levy for those rights. This was a matter of clear self-interest, since the barons and their fellows were much the most seriously affected by these financial exactions. Taxation for war could only be raised by consent, and arbitrary taxation was forbidden. Royal officials were to be subject to regulation and scrutiny and all were to know the content of the law and to act within it.

Three remarkable elements had major implications for the future, even if largely redundant at the time. First, the charter was designed to protect the interest of *liber homo*, the 'free man'. Not democratic in any modern sense, it was focused on a particular class in the social hierarchy, but this was defined more generously than elsewhere in Europe by including not only the barons and knights, but also the 'free tenants', those who would later be labelled as 'yeomen' and 'freeholders'. These people thus became part of the system, helping to undermine feudal structures and to produce the flexible social hierarchy which characterised later medieval England. Second, chapters 12 and 14 provided that certain taxation could only be levied by the king with the consent of the 'common counsel' (that is, the nobility, the ecclesiastical lords, and the tenants in chief or greater barons). While this, too, was a matter of blatant self-interest it had crucial implications, for it implied a defined consultative body with a regular and formal role in government. And third, the so-called 'Security Clause' (chapter 61) provided that a council of 25 barons would monitor and scrutinise the behaviour of the king and leading royal officials, checking on the implementation of the charter and with power to discipline the king and restrain his actions by seizing lands, castles and possessions, 'until, in their opinion, amends have been made'. In other words, the king was now to be subject to the law and leading subjects were empowered to act against him if he transgressed.

**The failure of Magna Carta**

All of this is powerful stuff, but the fact that eight centuries later we place such a high value upon it would certainly have seemed wildly implausible to the protagonists at Runnymede. The barons had no real sense of the long-term implications of a document hastily concocted to tie the hands of a troublesome and vexatious monarch, a document designed to bolster the interests of their own class and to enhance its role in government. And

John, notoriously, was duplicitous and slippery—he would do anything to buy time and make a breathing space. For him, agreeing to the charter was a meaningless expedient.

The document was ratified on 19 June and multiple copies were speedily produced and sent out to all cathedrals and possibly to major towns to publicise the king's submission. Four survive from what might originally have been several dozen: one is, of course, at Salisbury. But it seems likely that, in addition, orders were issued that the text should be read out in French and (crucially) in English at public gatherings. The original is in technical Latin, meaningless to most, but the early translation into the two spoken languages of the realm, those of the elite and of the common people, began the transformation of Magna Carta into a cornerstone of liberty.[4]

Within six weeks John had rejected and repudiated the charter. Its initial

Effigy of King John. Photograph by Mr Christopher Guy, Worcester Cathedral Archaeologist. Reproduced by permission of the Chapter of Worcester Cathedral (UK).

currency lasted little more than a month. His emissaries went straight to his new ally and supporter, Pope Innocent III, who on 24 August 2015 denounced and annulled the charter, describing it as 'not only shameful and demeaning, but also illegal and unjust ... lessening and impairing [the king's] rights and dignity' (which was of course the whole point). In mid-September three papal legates came to England to reiterate Innocent's words, condemning 'the despoiling of the king of his royal dignity'. The charter, unceremoniously ditched by the king and formally cancelled by the pope, was null and void.

Civil war broke out again in early September and the barons, confronted by an invigorated king who had thrown aside the shackles of Runnymede, faced defeat. John campaigned with determination and might have won outright had not Louis, the dauphin of France, invaded England on 21 May 1216 at the invitation of a faction of the barons. This foreign invasion—ironic indeed, since the charter demanded that the king should not employ foreign troops or mercenaries—was accompanied by incursions from Scotland. John fought on three fronts—against the French in the south, the Scots in the north, and the barons in the middle—and by October 1216 succeeded, against the odds, in stopping the progress of all his enemies. But at that crucial moment, exhausted by a year of hard fighting, he became critically ill while lodging at Newark-upon-Trent, and died there—perhaps from peritonitis—on the night of 19 October. Matthew Paris, typically hostile, attributed his death to depression and despondency, compounded by 'disgusting gluttony, for that night by indulging too freely in peaches and copious draughts of new cider he greatly increased his feverishness'.

## The success of Magna Carta

John's unanticipated early death—he was 50 years old—created a desperate crisis in a nation ravaged by civil war, with perhaps one-third of its territory in French hands. The new king, Henry III, was nine years old and it was absolutely imperative that his guardians, led by the great William Marshall, Earl of Pembroke, one of the towering figures of the medieval world, should win over the rebellious barons to support a new regime whose very survival was precarious in the extreme. On 12 November 2016 Magna Carta, cast aside fifteen months before, was resurrected, reissued and ratified by the advisers of the boy king as a signal to the barons that their interests would be protected and their status guaranteed. Louis the Dauphin eventually withdrew and on 12 September 1217 the Treaty of Kingston brought about peace between England and France. In early October 1217 Magna Carta was reissued for a second time, reminding the barons that they could place trust in the new government and that Henry's reign would be very different from that of his father. In effect, a form of constitutional settlement was achieved with Magna Carta as its centrepiece.

Thereafter, with frequent revisions and reissues, Magna Carta became a talismanic guarantee of liberties. Hundreds of copies were made over the ensuing decades, sent to boroughs and county sheriffs, cathedrals and great churches, and bodies such as the Duchy of Lancaster, read aloud in the vernacular and becoming a familiar image in courts of law and political gatherings. Within fifty years it was a standard point of reference in judicial cases, and in 1265 was sharply in the minds of the rebellious barons who, late in his long life and reign, fought against John's son Henry III and convened the first formally constituted English parliament. Its immortality was ensured.

### *A note on further reading*

For the background to the period and its politics, see Michael Clanchy, *England and its rulers 1066–1307* (3rd edition Blackwell, 2006) or David Carpenter, *The struggle for mastery: the political history of Britain 1066–1284* (Penguin, 2004). Richard Huscroft's *Ruling England 1042–1217* (Pearson Education, 2005) is a clear and very accessible introduction. *A social history of England 1200–1500* by Rosemary Horrox and Mark Ormrod (Cambridge University Press, 2006) provides context on the world in which Magna Carta was created and became embedded in national thinking. The definitive translation of and introduction to Magna Carta itself is David Carpenter's 2015 Penguin Classic edition. For the king himself, the most important biography (and political history of the reign and its context) is W L Warren, *King John* (Yale University Press, 1997), first written in the early 1960s but still impressive. Among other recent biographies, see Ralph V Turner, *King John: England's evil king* (1994 and reissued by The History Press, 2009).

### Notes

1   Green, J R, 1888, *A short history of the English people*, London, 122–123
2   Lodge, Eleanor C, 1926, *Gascony under English rule*, Methuen, 23
3   Tatton-Brown, Tim, 2007/8, 'Windsor Castle before 1348', *Annual Report of the Friends of St George's, Windsor*, 483-490. I am grateful to Tim Tatton-Brown for discussing this with me.
4   This question is discussed in Clanchy, M T, 2012, *From memory to written record: England 1066-1307*, 3rd edition Blackwell, 262-268

Seth Ward, Bishop of Salisbury, 1667–1689 © Salisbury Cathedral School

# 'Woman professing godliness': a 19th century resident of the College of Matrons

## Penelope Rundle

The survival of a little bundle of six letters among the records of the College of Matrons[1] gives us a rare picture of the life and misfortunes of one of the poorer 19th century inhabitants of the Close. She was called Jemima Butt and lived there for about 20 years until her death in 1867.

The College of Matrons was founded in 1682 by Bishop Seth Ward for widows from the diocese of Salisbury, or failing that from Exeter. They had to be over the age of 50 (nowadays it is 55). The original building is still in use, a row of small houses just inside the High Street gate of the Cathedral Close. It is much photographed by tourists, particularly the elaborate coats of arms over the front door; what they do not see is the beautiful quiet garden at the back.

Jemima Butt, née Hubbel or Hubbald (the spelling varies) was admitted to the College in 1847,[2] the widow of a Berkshire clergyman who had gone mad and died in an asylum. This was not her only misfortune. When Jemima was just four years old her parents went to America and died there, so she was brought up by relatives in Wolverhampton. She knew that she was born in Birmingham, but she was never able to trace her baptism, which before the days of civil registration was the accepted way to prove one's age. It has still not been found. However from later records she must have been born in 1792.[3]

Jemima's beautifully written letter of application shows that she had made the most of her education. She was also well grounded in the Christian faith

Extract from Jemima Butt's letter of application, (courtesy Salisbury Cathedral archives)
For a transcript see p 44-5

and a faithful member of the Church of England wherever she lived. All this, with the continuing care and concern of her relatives in later life, suggests that as a child she had a stable and happy upbringing.

It was probably in 1822 that Jemima married a widower, the Rev John Marten Butt, rector of East Garston in Berkshire. At that time his parish was in the diocese of Salisbury. The diocese has had a complicated history: until 1542 it consisted of the three counties of Wiltshire, Dorset and Berkshire. In 1542 Dorset was moved to Bristol diocese, but returned to Salisbury at the same time as Berkshire was moved to Oxford. So by the skin of her teeth Jemima was eligible as the widow of a clergyman in the diocese of Salisbury.

Her husband came from a clerical family. He was born in 1774, the son of the Rev George Butt DD and his wife Martha Sherwood. He was always known by his second name, Marten. We know quite a bit about his early life from the memoir of his sister Mary Martha.[4] As Mrs M M Sherwood (she married a cousin) she was celebrated in her day as the author of a number of extremely pious and improving tales for children; the best known of these is *The Fairchild Family*.[5]

As a boy Marten was sent to Dr Valpy's school at Reading and from there to Westminster School before going to Christ Church, Oxford. He was a scholarly young man with wide interests. His sister Mary says that in one vacation he 'instructed me in botany and persuaded me to learn Greek. He taught me the verbs when walking out, and put me at once into Homer, and I continued the study until I had read the first six books.'[6] In 1802 Marten was presented to the living of East Garston, which he retained until his death.[7]

Marten's first marriage, in 1806, was to Mary Ann Congreve, a childhood friend of his sister Mary. They lived in his other parish of Oddingley in Worcestershire. The first child was born there in 1807 and other children quickly followed. Mary Ann died in 1818 giving birth to their eighth child, Theophilus, who lived only long enough to be baptised. So in his early forties John Marten Butt was left with seven motherless children, the oldest of whom cannot have been more than eleven years old. At first they were distributed among his two sisters, Mary and Lucy, but this was probably only a temporary arrangement.[8]

Left a widower, Marten made a fresh start and moved to East Garston. His marriage to Jemima is likely to have been in 1822, as their eldest child, another Jemima, was born in 1823.[9] This marriage may well have been an arrangement that suited them both. Jemima had few prospects. She was 30 years old, with no independent income and no hope of any inheritance. As the rector's wife she would gain both security and a well respected place in society. In the event she proved to be a faithful and steadfast wife and mother over many years.

Three more children were born during the couple's time at East Garston. Eleanor, born in October 1824, died in March 1825 at the age of seven months.[10] Then came the only boy, William Boyne, who grew up to follow the family tradition and train as a doctor. And finally Emily Martha Whittingham was born in East Garston in 1827. It appears that as Marten's illness took hold he had to relinquish parish duties: the last entries by him in the parish registers of East Garston are a burial in February 1830 and a baptism in March 1830.[11]

So perhaps he and Jemima were staying with friends for a while when their youngest child, Matilda, was born in 1831 in Oystermouth, near Swansea.[12]

From 1830 the curate who had looked after the parish of East Garston before Marten's arrival now took over again, though Marten retained the freehold. There is one last glimpse of Marten, probably shortly before he had to be confined. His sister came over to Bridgnorth in Shropshire to visit him and Jemima. Mary tells us that as she was leaving:

> I looked back and back from the carriage to gaze on him as long as I could see him;   he was walking on under the rock, Mrs. Butt holding his arm . . . his person was bent,     and the wind agitated his thin white hair.[13]

In 1833 he had to be admitted to the Oulton Retreat for the Reception of Lunatics, a privately run asylum near Stone in Staffordshire. It probably existed between the 1830s and the 1870s, but no records have survived.[14] Marten is recorded there in the 1841 census return and remained until his death.[15]

So Jemima was left on her own to care for a large brood of young children. One of Marten's older sons, visiting the rectory in 1833, complained to his brother:

> I am far from well and cannot bear the noise of this family. The house is as full as it can hold, the rooms small and the heat and noise is more than I can bear . . . there are ten children at home; you may suppose what a scene of turmoil there is when they are all in the parlour, there is scarcely room to move about.[16]

The occasion for this visit was Jemima's sale of the entire contents of the rectory. This was bitterly opposed by the family but they were too late to prevent it. And Jemima badly needed the money, not for herself but for her husband. The rectory house had to be repaired and newly furnished before the curate could move in; part of the income of the benefice had to be used for the curate's stipend; and Marten's asylum fees had to be paid. Although the contents of the house were enough for a three day sale, in the event they only raised £300 because they were in such poor condition. Someone has written at the end of the inventory 'A great many items throughout the inventory entirely rubbish.' The only valuable item was Marten's library of over 800 books, including theology, history, classical works, science, poetry and biography. At the front is a list of the ten books he asked to keep with him at the asylum, including Greek, Hebrew and English bibles.[17]

Jemima may have chosen a Staffordshire asylum in order to keep her husband as near to her as possible. She had returned to her childhood home of Wolverhampton and in 1841 she is recorded as living in Clarendon Street. With her she had the two youngest children, thirteen year old Emily and ten year old Matilda.[18] We know from Jemima's testimonials that she made every effort, on a very limited income, to provide her husband with some small comforts while he was detained. He died in 1846.[19]

Before Jemima was admitted to the College of Matrons in 1847 there was a severe strain on her finances. Not only were the two girls still dependent on her, but her son was training as a doctor and would have no income until he could set up in a practice of his own. We know that Matilda lived with her mother at least until 1851, when she was twenty,[20] but she does not appear there in the 1861 census return.

Rather more is known of Emily. In 1854 she married an Indian Army officer, Henry Daniel Maunsell,[21] and went out to India. Perhaps she met her husband through her aunt Mary's Indian connections. In any case in 1861 she was back in Salisbury, visiting her mother.[22] With her she had a five year old son who was born in India and had the curious first name of Debonnaire, probably a family surname. It seems highly likely that he was

Bell-pull, 43 the Close (photo Roy Bexon)

to be left in England when his mother returned to India. During the Raj it was customary for small children to be sent home at about five years old – exactly the same thing happened to Rudyard Kipling, who had a wretched childhood with paid guardians in Southsea. [23] But any child who remained in India ran a very high risk of yellow fever and other tropical diseases, and many died. One can only hope that young Debonnaire found as loving a home as his grandmother did in her own childhood.

For about a year before her move to Salisbury Jemima lived in London, perhaps because her son was training there. Her place of worship was the Church of England chapel in Charlotte Street, Pimlico in the parish of St. George's, Hanover Square. [24] During her time in London she evidently retained regular links with her own family in Staffordshire and with at least one friend of her late husband, for they provided the necessary testimonials as to her age and her financial status. Perhaps also it was one of them who brought her to the notice of the Bishop of Oxford when at last she was free to move to Salisbury.

The College of Matrons minute book which records Jemima Butt's election includes a note of the rather unusual circumstances:

> Jemima Butt, widow of the Revd J M Butt Rector of East Garston Berks (formerly in the diocese of Sarum) was elected December 1847 – it being considered that Mr Butt having been an incumbent in Berkshire before the severance of that County from the diocese of Sarum and its annexation to that of Oxford, his widow was admissible to this College – nominated by the Bishop.
> A note below adds 'Died 5 March 1867.' [25]

So what would life have been like for Jemima in the College of Matrons? She would at least have had something in common with the other clergy widows. Unlike the 'deserving poor' for whom the rest of the Salisbury charities were founded, the residents of the College were considered gentlefolk – though certainly poor. Some would even have had a servant sleeping up in the attic (the house now called 43 The Close has kept its bell-pull to the right of the fireplace).

But conditions were pretty cramped. The houses each side of the main passage had five rooms each, as they still do: two on the ground floor, two bedrooms and an attic. But the RCHM reconstruction thinks that the other eight had only one room on the ground floor, and some had shared staircases up to the first floor. [26] By the time of Jemima's death there was such dissatisfaction that the Trustees were having difficulty in filling the places and there were only six residents out of a possible ten. [27] This led to major alterations and reconstruction in 1870. The architect was T H Wyatt. The original eight smaller houses were converted to six, with a new one then added at each end on the garden side. More windows were made and the shared staircases done away with. [28]

That is the building as we see it today: but not as Jemima knew it. One would love to know which house she lived in, but there is no record.

In many ways conditions in the 1850s were not much different from those set out in Bishop Seth Ward's deed of 1683, though the original allowance of six shillings a week for each Matron had been increased to £10 a quarter. Each of the women had her own plot in the communal garden, but was expected to share a privy and the laundry. The laundry room still survives, with the original brick floor, an enormous copper and a lead pump dated 1713.

It is said that at one time the Matrons were expected to wash the surplices and other linen of the Cathedral clergy and choir, but fortunately this has fallen into abeyance.

Of course some rules of conduct had to be observed, for the good of the community and its reputation. The Matrons were forbidden to have a lodger, or to be away for more than a month in the year. If they went outside the gates of the Close they were always to have a companion. And they were to be regular daily attenders at services in the Cathedral, since that was their parish church. [29] One hopes that Jemima was able to settle into this new life in the College of Matrons, and that she enjoyed peace and security after the anxiety and stress of her previous situation over many years.

*Opposite*: Matrons' College, rear aspect from gardens (photo Roy Bexon)

Lead pump dated 1713 (photo Roy Bexon)

At the end of their lives many of the Matrons were not buried in Salisbury; probably they chose to be buried with their late husbands or their families elsewhere. But Jemima chose differently. Her early ties with Staffordshire must now have seemed far away (she was 74). And her husband had spent a quarter of a century in an asylum while she struggled on her own. She chose to be buried in the Close, which had been her home for almost twenty years. The funeral took place on 9 March 1867. Usually the officiant would have been either the Sub-Dean or the Vicar of the Close, but Jemima had arranged a reminder of her London days: the ceremony was performed by Stanley Leather, Preacher and Assistant Minister, St. James, Piccadilly.[30] Her remains lie in the north-east quarter of the cloister garth, in plot No 24, almost opposite the entrance to the Chapter House.[31]

There is much that we will never know about Jemima Butt, partly because of the obscurity of her origins. But she may stand for all the women who for more than 330 years have found both security and independence in Seth Ward's College of Matrons. Many might have equally interesting stories to tell, if only we knew.

## Testimonial letters

My Lord,

I beg to certify that I have known Mrs. Jemima Butt since the year 1796 at which time she was four years old, and being a relative of my father's was then adopted into our family, in consequence of her own parents going to America where they both died. If the exercise of every Christian duty and trials borne with exemplary patience can entitle the widow of a truly pious and learned clergyman to the benefit of your excellent charity I know no one that can be more deserving of it.

I am, My Lord, your obedient servant, Eleanor Devey. October 23rd, 1847. St. Paul's Terrace, Wolverhampton.

★★★★

Oxford, October 25, 1847.

My Lord, I hope you will not think me guilty of an impropriety in offering to your Lordship my testimony respecting Mrs. Butt, the widow of the Revd. J.M. Butt (late incumbent of East Garston), a friend with whom I was intimately acquainted from the time we were at School together at Westminster, till the period when his mind became deranged, some years before his death. Having been well acquainted with Mrs. Butt during the last thirty years, I can with truth say, that in all those relations of life which she has been called to fulfil, her conduct has been most exemplary, more particularly during the period of her husband's derangement, throughout which period, at the same time as she fulfilled all the duties of a mother in attending to the religious education of her children, one son and three daughters, she curtailed the expenses of herself and family to the utmost, in order to afford her husband all the comforts in her power, which his unhappy situation required.

I remain, My Lord, with great respect, your Lordship's most obedient servant. J. Kidd.

We the undersigned, being the Incumbent and Curate of St. George's Church, Wolverhampton, do readily certify that Mrs. Butt, while residing in Wolverhampton, was an exemplary attendant of St. George's Church. Her general conduct was not only unexceptionable, while she resided here, but she was such as to merit the sympathy and esteem of all who could appreciate 'what becometh woman professing godliness'.

G.B.C. Cave, Incumbent of St. George's, Wolverhampton. W.A. Newman, MA, Curate of St. George's. October 19th, 1847.

★★★★

Mrs. Butt, widow of the Revd. John Martin Butt, has attended this Chapel for the last twelvemonth and it has given me sincere pleasure to learn that she has now met with an opening into the Widows' College, New Sarum. I am quite satisfied from my knowledge of her religious habits and character and the testimony I am familiar with from all quarters of her uniform respectability, that all requirements on this head for admission to the benefits of the institution will be fully answered by her.

James Kelly (?), Minister of Charlotte Chapel, Pimlico. October 25th, 1847.

★★★★

I hereby certify that the income of Mrs. Jemima Butt, widow of the Reverend John Marten Butt, lately amounted to the sum of £51. 11. 6 a year, but that she has now agreed out of the same to give up, absolutely, the sum of £12 a year to two of her daughters: Emily Martha Whittingham Butt and Matilda Butt. And I further certify that I have acted as solicitor for Mrs. Butt, and consider myself to be acquainted with the nature and extent of her income; and I verily believe she has no other income, except from the Widows' Relief Charity, than the income above mentioned, which does not amount to £40 a year.

Frederick Nicholls Devey, Ely Palace, London. 25th October 1847

★★★★

**Transcript of Jemima Butt's letter**
1 Trelleck Terrace, Pimlico, London.
My Lord,
Having understood from the Bishop of Oxford that you would be so kind as to endeavour to procure admission for me into the Widows' College in case my testimonials should be satisfactory, I beg leave to submit the accompanying for your approbation. The copy of the baptismal register I have not been able to obtain from the circumstance of being separated very young from my parents

and I cannot learn at what church my name was entered. I therefore hope that your Lordship will feel satisfied as to my age from the testimony of a relative with whom I resided in my youth. The two daughters upon whom I have settled the £12 per annum named in Mr. Devey's certificate are entirely dependent upon me for their maintenance, and in addition I have to support my son while he is qualifying for the medical profession from which he can obtain no employment for three years. Your Lordship will judge from these circumstances how very grateful I should be if you can favour my reception. I am, My Lord, your obedient servant, Jemima Butt. October 25th, 1847.

## Bibliography

*Dictionary of National Biography*, 2004, Oxford University Press.

Royal Commission on the Historical Monuments of England, 1993, *Salisbury: the Houses of the Close*, London HMSO.

*Brief Account of the Charity Called the College of Matrons*, Salisbury, Bennett Brothers, 1879.

Eward, Suzanne M, *Seth Ward's Widows*, 'Spire', Friends of Salisbury Cathedral, 1982.

Sherwood, M M, 1854, *The Life of Mrs. Sherwood, chiefly autobiographical, edited by her daughter, Sophia Kelly*, London: Darton and Co., Holborn Hill.

## Notes

1   College of Matrons records in Salisbury Cathedral archives. (CM)
2   CM minute book
3   CM letter of Eleanor Devey, 1847
4   Sherwood, M M, 1854, *The Life of Mrs. Sherwood, chiefly autobiographical, edited by her daughter, Sophia Kelly*, London: Darton and Co., Holborn Hill
5   *Dictionary of National Biography*, 2004, Oxford University Press, vol 50, 345
6   Sherwood. 1854, 163
7   The Berkshire Echo: The Newsletter of the Berkshire Record Office, No.3 Autumn 1997, 1
8   Sherwood. 1854, 524, 525
9   Berkshire Record Office (BRO). D/P59/1/5
10  BRO, D/P59/1/8
11  BRO, D/P59/1/8.5
12  1851 Census HO 107/1846/93
13  Sherwood. 1854, 566
14  Information from the Staffordshire and Stoke on Trent Archive Service
15  1841 Census HO 107/995/10
16  BRO, D/EZ/106/3/7
17  BRO, D/EZ/106/3/7
18  1841 Census HO 107/1000/9
19  CM letter of J. Kidd, 1847
20  1851 Census HO/107/1846  93
21  Civil registration, Alderbury 5a 303

22  1861 Census RG/9/1315  18

23  *Dictionary of National Biography*, 2004, vol 31  749

24  CM letter of James Kelly, 1847

25  CM minute book

26  Royal Commission on the Historical Monuments of England, 1993, *Salisbury: The Houses of the Close*, London, HMSO, 153, 154

27  *Brief Account of the Charity Called the College of Matrons*, Salisbury, Bennett Brothers, 1879, 11

28  CM plans of Matrons' College by T H Wyatt, 1870

29  Eward, Suzanne M, *Seth Ward's Widows*, 'Spire', Friends of Salisbury Cathedral, 1982

30  Salisbury Cathedral burial register, in the Cathedral Library

31  Spring, R O C, register of floor slabs and cloister garth burials, in the Cathedral Library

# Tales of the Riverbank: West Harnham in the 15th century (WSA 4258)

## Steven Hobbs

'I've got something which may interest you', the voice said over the telephone, 'medieval scrolls, chalk rolls, dating from 1347. They were handed to me twenty five years ago having been found in a stone sarcophagus in the crypt of a redundant church in Salisbury'. Despite the rather fantastic provenance of the documents with a Da Vinci Codesque element, something caught my attention. The definite date added some credence; furthermore there was a manor and hundred of Chalke in south Wiltshire, which could explain the perplexing phrase. Expressing interest and barely disguising the level to which I was intrigued we arranged for the documents to be collected by a colleague who would be in Salisbury the following week.

As soon as the 'scrolls' were examined their importance was evident. What had come into our hands was a most significant collection, in excellent condition, of manor court rolls, accounts and surveys not only for various manors in central and south Wiltshire, but also running into Dorset, Gloucestershire, and reaching as far as Northamptonshire and East Sussex. Each roll had an adhesive label of the type used to send unwrapped printed material through the post with name and date written in ink. There was no obvious link between them of a single manorial overlord, lay or monastic; they were an entirely artificial accumulation presumably brought together by a collector as one might have collected rare books, coins or stamps. For that reason the documents are being distributed to the appropriate local archive services.

Two clues as to their provenance were immediately apparent. In 1959 we had received a similar collection, including some material from manors represented here, from the widow of the grandson of Henry James Fowle Swayne. He was Recorder of Wilton until 1885, and his antiquarian interests led him to research extensively the history of Wilton and Salisbury. He must have found a kindred spirit in C R Straton, his son in law, which could only have eased the younger man's reception into the family. Straton edited the Pembroke estate survey of 1565 published by the Roxburghe Club in 1909. He was the Medical Officer of Health for Wilton RDC, and a number of records of that post, held after him by Alex Straton, were found with the manorial records, which only served to consolidate this provenance.

And what of the Wiltshire documents? They include the earliest examples of manor court rolls (for Urchfont from 1262), manorial accounts (again for Urchfont, 1265, but also the Wilton abbey manors of Overton, Stanton St Bernard and North Newnton for 1294-5, and also of hundredal court rolls (Chalke from 1339) in the collections of Wiltshire and Swindon Archives (WSA), making it one of our most significant collections of medieval archives.

However, the most interesting series are court rolls of the manor of West Harnham, View of Frankpledge, 1411–36, and Court Leet 1416-35. They are the most informative and the longest run among the cache. A brief examination of them revealed several details of considerable topographical interest. There are frequent references to *Lawediche*, part of which described

*Above*: (4258/1/12) The fishermen poachers, Nov 1426 court leet, Nov 1416
*Opposite*: (4258/1/11) Matter involving the prior of Ivychurch, Nov 1416 View of Frankpledge

as running between the farm and Netherhampton was called *Brodemere*. This is thought by Tim Tatton-Brown to refer to the straight western boundary of West Harnham from the Nadder to the top of the Down. A cross mentioned in 1423 on the western boundary, Tim believes, must have stood on the main road to Netherhampton. A ditch called *le Ryde*, a footbridge at *Stonhulle*, a way to *Triponscrofte*, and *Crouchlane*, all provide further clues as to the topography of the manor.

In November 1416 Walter Rowde, the prior of Ivychurch, attended the court to affirm his right to a close of land adjoining the house formerly of Edward de Harnham on the western boundary of West Harnham above the highway. Its bounds are recorded in great detail. It ran between a field of David Cervynton called *Hogkynsham* on the west and the principal house formerly of John Kirkeby, then of Oliver de Harnham, on the east; its boundary from the highway continued south along an ancient ditch up to a newly built wall between the two granges, one of which lay in the disputed close. Its route was then described in relation to an oak called *Twsyllidok*, the stump (*stirpitem*) of an elder tree and a couple of poplar trees. The 12-strong jury (all named) found in favour of the prior.

The many minor misdemeanours and infringements for which individuals were frequently presented at the court are revealing of the tensions within this riparian manor and add to our knowledge about life in medieval Wiltshire. At the Hockday court in April 1415 John Lupeyate was in mercy for allowing the footpath called *Wyntersherd* by the weir to become miry and broken up to the detriment of everyone. In Nov 1415 he was presented for allowing the bridge on the Fisherton bank and the gates of the weir to become weakened and damaged.

At the same court William Ledys (*Ledus*), the lord's miller, was presented for blocking the weir of the mill causing the water to flood onto the tenements of the tenants of the manor. He was accused of unjustly taking toll, for the use of the mill, from several persons (one of whom might have been John Corslegh who was charged, at the same court, with drawing a dagger on William). This was something William was regularly presented for and the infringement, for which a fine of 12d was regularly imposed, seems to have been regarded as a licence, making sure that it was registered and paid for. However, at the same Hockday court in 1415 he faced much sterner opposition from a jury of 12 named men who accused him of being a breaker and disturber of the peace; his wife Alice was a scold (*garrulatrix*); he had stolen poultry of neighbours of William de Harnham, namely chickens, geese and piglets; he had also caused damage by taking four piles (stakes) from the mill; also a tool (*instrum*) weighing 7lbs and worth 21d, a measure of half bushel, a stone, a *toldyssh* (toll dish into which tolls were paid), a basket, and a *mullebytell* (a beetle or mallet specifically for use in a mill) worth 22d, belonging to Oliver Cervynton,[1] lord of West Harnham; they also claimed that William had broken the planks of the mill and damaged its 'Flodyates'; furthermore he had turned a blind eye to the several men who fished in the river without the permission of the lord. No further action appears to have been taken, but the clear impression is given that he was a difficult and tricky man, not averse to resorting to threats with a sword and staff when challenged, as appears from an earlier court appearance.

The court rolls provide interesting evidence of the fulling mill in West Harnham. In 1421 John Benet, *mullward* (millwright), was accused of taking a cart of timber from it; while in 1417 a dozen green cloths belonging to Thomas Wake were distrained in payment for the fulling of his cloths in the mill.

In April 1430 Hugh Mildemay, a hellier from Salisbury, was presented that on 6 December he had taken two cygnets, each worth 40d, belonging to John Franks and Edward Prentis, from the lord's waters of *Swepole*; furthermore on the same day he took six geese, worth 12d, belonging to

John Benet, millward, above the causeway of West Harnham that reaches beyond Fisherton mill. He had also taken a 'storepot' belonging to John, which was submerged in the water and held an eel, worth 12d and six more eels, worth 6d, and a trout, worth12d, in the same pot. All these were taken by force of arms and against the king's peace; the tithing was ordered to arrest him.

One of the most significant aspects of the court rolls is the ecological evidence about the river Nadder, which appeared to support a wide variety of fish. The most common offence was infringing the lord's rights of fishing; in short poaching. In 1431 John Gebeis, senior and junior, and Ralph Gebeis were presented for attempting to drag the lord's waters in the river from *le Were* as far as *Swepole, Briggepole* and *les Flodyates* using a net called a *Bastardtramulle* which was described as an illegal net from which no fish can escape. In April 1417 several men were presented for taking trout, grayling (*humbros*) and other fish, namely minnows or small fry (*menuse*), valued at 16s.

In 1425 John Benet, the shady millwright mentioned above, and John Gibbus used nets and other trickery to take trout and grayling. Others used various nets called *Tramyl, Wade, Dacenet* and *Shosnettes* to take a wide variety of fish including trout, eels, dace, and grayling. In November 1434 two men were fined for each using a *Trowthtspere* and *hooknettes*. The use of words meaning small fish (*memise* and *pisciculos*, and *ep(h)emora*) indicate an awareness of the lord's officials of the need to protect and sustain future fish stocks. While this was motivated by the aim to protect the interests of the lord of the manor, nevertheless, it has a resonance with contemporary concerns about the decline in the numbers and variety of fish in our rivers and oceans.

The emergence of these documents is a cause of much excitement among archivists both at the Wiltshire and Swindon History Centre and further afield. Such feelings will be shared by Salisbury historians, albeit tinged by a little frustration that they were unavailable for the contributors to *Harnham Historical Miscellany*, published in 2013 in memory of Michael Cowan. However, we all must be grateful for the generosity of the depositor presenting them as a gift to the History Centre, where they are available for researchers, present and future.

**Notes**

1   Oliver Cervington held the manor of West Harnham until his death in 1419/20 when the title passed to his son, David Cervington (died 1456). Manorial Documents Register (MDR) draft authority file for West Harnham and Britford per Virginia Bainbridge.

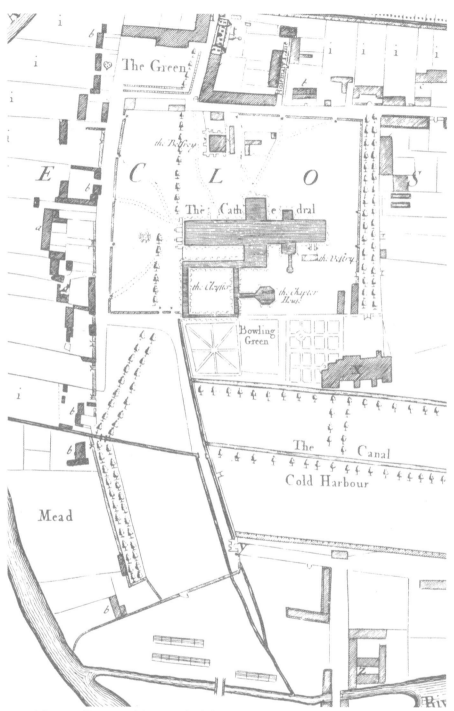

Detail from William Naish's map of Salisbury (c1720). Leadenhall lies between the water channel on the north and the 'Mead' beside the South Canonry garden

# The Gardens of The Leadenhall 70 The Close, Salisbury

## Tim Tatton-Brown

The Leadenhall, in the south-western part of the Close of Salisbury Cathedral, was one of the earliest of the canons' houses to be built. It was put up as a model canon's house some time in the 1220s,[1] by Elias de Dereham, who was the 'Rector of the Fabric' and probably the designer of Salisbury Cathedral.[2] The last visible fragment of this house, the south-east wing, was sadly demolished in 1915, though some of the masonry of the early 13th century doors and windows was saved and rebuilt in a wall on the south-east side of the present house. Today the building is home to the girls and staff of Leaden Hall School.

The house was completely rebuilt in about 1720 by Canon Edward Talbot (Treasurer, and Archdeacon of Berkshire), and again in about 1800 by Canon William Douglas (Precentor, and Archdeacon of Wiltshire), though the southern part of the house may well contain medieval walls within it.[3] The present landscaped gardens around Leadenhall must have been laid out in Canon Douglas' time, in the first few years of the 19th century. The main boundary walls, as well as the overall topographical features, must also date from this time, as no doubt do the very mature trees in the grounds. Twenty years or so after this, John Constable visited and stayed at Leadenhall with his great friend Canon John Fisher (Archdeacon of Berkshire), and the grounds around Leadenhall are depicted in many of Constable's sketches and paintings made in 1820 and 1829.[4]

Archdeacons William Douglas and John Fisher both got their positions and houses from their relatives, Bishops of Salisbury. Fisher's uncle was Bishop from 1807 to 1825, and he succeeded Dr John Douglas (Bishop

1791–1807), the father of William Douglas. John Douglas was a remarkable self-made man, born on 14 July 1721, who became Bishop of Carlisle (1787–91) and Dean of Windsor (1788–91) before being translated to Salisbury.[5] His son the Revd William Douglas, who was known as Mr 'Chancellor' Douglas (Chancellor of the diocese, not the cathedral) was a very wealthy man because of the patronage of his father. Apart from being a canon residentiary of Salisbury Cathedral he held the prebends of Combe and Harnham (from 1792) and Fordington (from 1800). He was also the Archdeacon of Wiltshire, from 1799, when he moved to Leadenhall, and Warden of St Nicholas' Hospital in Salisbury, as well as Rector of Brixton Deverell and Vicar of Potterne (both rich livings in Wiltshire). He was, finally, also a Canon of Westminster Abbey (1807–18), where he completely rebuilt his residence, now No 17 Dean's Yard, in 1808–9. Thus he may be seen as an 'Archdeacon Grantly' figure, as so brilliantly depicted by Anthony Trollope a generation later.

As soon as William Douglas was established at Leadenhall in 1799, where he succeeded Canon Nathaniel Hume (1772–99),[6] he started to reconstruct the house with a new 'Gothic' exterior and 'Classical' interior. Externally the whole house was covered in a thick layer of stucco, made to look like stone ashlar-work, with imitation joints and tooling.[7] Around this very grand house a new series of spaces was created, most of which survive after over two centuries. These different features will now be briefly described though, unfortunately, no documentary evidence for their construction seems to have survived. The grounds are very accurately represented on the Ordnance Survey first edition 1:500 maps of Salisbury of 1880,[8] and the semi-mature landscape of these maps can be closely compared with the present situation nearly140 years later.

Leadenhall had two entrances from the West Walk of the Cathedral Close; a way in, on the north-east, to a stable yard and a grand entry to the front courtyard on the east, through a cast-iron gateway. This gateway is said to have been widened by Canon Douglas so that H R H the Prince of Wales (later George IV) could sweep into the grounds at speed in his carriage and four.[9] The front gravelled courtyard is still today in the form in which it was laid out at the beginning of the 19th century, with a wide turning circle for carriages centred on the porch. On the north side of the courtyard is a large archway leading into the stable yard, and all this is clearly shown in Buckler's pencil sketch of the courtyard, looking west, made in about 1810.[10]

Only the two pairs of stone bollards on the eastern side of the gravel turning area are now missing. On the north-east and south-east sides of the courtyard are grass lawns (the small flower beds are more recent) which

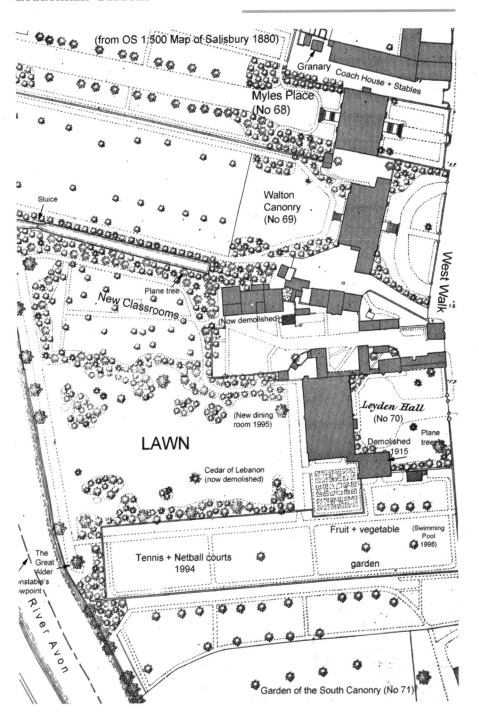

Detail, with annotations, from the Ordnance Survey 1:500 plan of Salisbury (published 1880) showing Leadenhall gardens (photograph Roy Bexon)

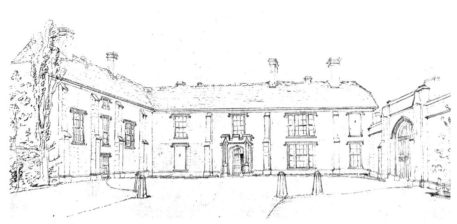

E J Buckler's pencil sketch of the east side of Leadenhall in c1810. Reproduced with permission from Wiltshire Museum, Devizes

allowed an uninterrupted view of the front of Leadenhall, through the iron railings from the West Walk. The public could, therefore, watch while grand personages like the Prince of Wales drove up to see Mr 'Chancellor' Douglas. In the south-east corner of the courtyard is an immense London plane tree, which was almost certainly planted soon after 1800, at a time when the planting of plane trees was common in England.[11] The Salisbury Close has several other large plane trees planted at about the same time, including three very fine specimens, not far away, that lie along the south-eastern boundary of the South Canonry, No 71.

The stable-yard area, north of the front courtyard of Leadenhall itself, was an integral part of the whole complex, but will not be described here as several of the buildings have been adapted or removed.[12] The west side of this yard contained the kitchen range and yard, as well as several other small service buildings which have also been demolished.[13] The bottom part of the brick wall, which surrounded this courtyard on the south-west, can just be seen at ground level immediately to the north of the great copper beech tree (see below).

Along the south side of the property, and stretching almost the whole way from the West Walk to the River Avon, was the fruit and vegetable (kitchen) garden. It is surrounded by contemporary walls,[14] and running across the full length of the kitchen garden from east to west was the main gravel walk. It had doors in the garden walls at either end of this walk. In recent years most of the area of the kitchen garden has been taken up by new facilities for the school, without damaging the surrounding walls. These comprise the tennis and netball courts (made in 1994) that occupy most of the western area, and a swimming pool (1998) in the south-east corner. A line of old apple trees still survives along the southern side of these fruit and vegetable gardens, as well as a few other apple trees and a white lilac in the north-eastern part of the garden.[15]

Between the southern end of the main house and the kitchen gardens is another small enclosed formal garden, with a yew hedge on its west side. This garden now contains a series of nine circles made from clipped box hedges, and the nine-fold division of the garden is also shown on the OS 1880 plan.[16] Along the southern side of this small garden the surrounding brick wall is interrupted by an iron railing on a low brick wall (allowing a view through into the fruit and vegetable garden), and there is a beautiful oil painting by John Constable of this garden (with the railing in the foreground) from the first floor window of Fisher's library in Leadenhall. In the distance is a fine view across the open garden of the South Canonry to Harnham hill in the background.[17]

The largest and most splendid space in the Leadenhall gardens runs west from the main front of the house to the River Avon. In the centre of this area is a large lawn with the remains of very mature shrubberies on its

The grand entry gate on the east side of Leadenhall in 2015 (photograph Roy Bexon)

John Constable. 'A View at Salisbury from Archdeacon Fisher's house'. Looking south to the 'Mead' at the south canonry from the first floor window in Leadenhall in 1820. Oil on canvas. ©Victoria & Albert Museum

north and south sides. These shrubberies were planted in a sinuous form that is well shown on the OS 1880 plan. The mature trees, of the early 19th century, that survive are mainly yews with hollies, box and some laurel. On the north-west side is a large evergreen oak, while on the north-east side, close to the kitchen yard wall, is a large copper beech and another very large London plane. Some trees (holly, box etc) were removed from the extreme north-east corner of the shrubbery when the new dining room (conservatory) was built in the spring of 1995. Standing in the middle of the south side of the lawn was a magnificent cedar of Lebanon which must also

*Opposite*: John Dunthorne the Younger. 'Salisbury cathedral'. Copy of the painting above. In a letter written to Archdeacon Fisher, from Hampstead, on 26 August 1827, John Constable tells him that 'John Dunthorne has completed a very pretty picture of your lawn and prebendal house with the great alder and cathedral'. Dunthorne was at this time a competent artist as well as Constable's very useful studio assistant. His death, and Fisher's death, both in 1832, left Constable devastated, and a lonely man. © The Fitzwilliam Museum, Cambridge. PD.24–1997

John Constable. 'Salisbury Cathedral and Leadenhall from the River Avon'. A view north-east from the Harnham watermeadows of the gardens at Leadenhall with family figures. A Lombardy poplar and the 'Great Alder' frame the spire. 1820. © The National Gallery, London

John Constable. 'Harnham Ridge and the Water Meadows from Fisher's Library'. View south-west across the garden with the great alder on the left and Harnham Hill beyond, with figures of the Constable and Fisher families on the river bank. Date 1820 or 1829. Oil on paper. © Victoria & Albert Museum, London

have been planted at the beginning of the 19th century.[18] Sadly it has very recently been cut down, but in Constable's time it was probably a small tree, similar to the cedars that can now be seen on the north-east side of Salisbury Cathedral, in the churchyard.[19]

Constable drew and painted quite a few views across the main lawn in 1820 and perhaps in 1829, and some of these views seem to show the then small cedar tree.[20] The most famous view across the garden, however, is his great unfinished oil on canvas 'Salisbury Cathedral and Leadenhall from the River Avon', made in the summer of 1820, now in the National Gallery. This was painted from the opposite side of the river and shows the Constable and Fisher families in the garden.[21] A much less well known copy of this view, now in the Fitzwilliam Museum, was made by Constable's pupil, John Dunthorne.

The shrubbery along the south side of the main lawn turns the corner at its south-west end, and runs for a short distance behind the west wall of the kitchen garden (see OS 1880 plan). There are several straggly yews here, but at the centre of this area, and at the southern end of the long riverside walk was the 'Great Alder' as Constable called it, surrounded by a garden seat. This is clearly shown in the famous oil painting mentioned above. Remarkably there is still an alder here, and this is probably a regrowth from the stool of the large tree of the 1820s.[22] Running north along the river bank from the 'Great Alder', the 1880 OS plan shows a broad terrace walk.

This was probably of gravel, and is shown in Constable's painting. It is not visible today having been grassed over, though there is still a change of slope here with a grass bank leading down to the river edge, and a more recent pollarded willow. Across the river from here is a hedgerow of pollarded trees, which Constable painted in 1820. This superb painting beautifully depicts the reflections in the foreground and shows the buildings of Harnham in the distance. The hedgerow and more recent pollards are still there (see overleaf).

The final section of the garden is the large area on the north-west between the old stable-yard and the river. It now contains temporary classrooms in an equally mature landscape of trees. Along the northern side of this is a modern fence which defines the boundary with the gardens of the Walton Canonry to the north. Earlier, however, the boundary here was marked by a stone-lined channel taking water from the River Avon on the west (there was a sluice here) to the bishop's garden on the east.[23]

Sadly this channel had been allowed to silt up and, more recently, it has been filled in. The stone-lined channel is clearly depicted on the 1880 OS plan, where its southern (Leadenhall) side is shown well screened by trees. There are still many mature trees here, particularly yews, and in the north-east corner is yet another very large London plane tree. The river walk is also shown running along the west side of this garden in the 1880 plan, and other narrower paths can be seen in this area which may, in part, have been used as a 'Pleasure Ground', as existed in the garden of the Bishop's Palace. There are also some sinuous shrubberies along the west and south sides of this area.[24]

Although changes have been made to the garden landscapes at Leadenhall,

View of Leadenhall and the cathedral from the Harnham watermeadows in 2015 (photograph Roy Bexon)

John Constable.'Watermeadows near Salisbury'.View across the Harnham watermeadows from Leadenhall garden, with reflected pollarded trees in the foreground, and Harnham church and mill beyond. 1820 (or 1829). Oil on canvas. ©Victoria& Albert Museum

The same view as above in 1995, with newly cut pollard (photograph Tim Tatton-Brown)

there are still large areas that can be compared directly with many of John Constable's sketches and paintings made there almost 200 years ago. Also, with the help of the painstakingly detailed Ordnance Survey map of 1879–80, it is possible to reconstruct accurately the places from which the pictures were made. John Constable is arguably England's greatest landscape painter, and thanks to his very close friendship with Archdeacon John Fisher we have a wonderful window into a garden of the Close in the 1820s, with Constable's exquisite depictions of the Harnham watermeadows beyond and the cloudscapes above. We are exceptionally fortunate to have here in Salisbury a rare, if not unique, opportunity to see the relationship between the artist and his subject.

**Acknowledgements**: with thanks to Leaden Hall School for access to their grounds. Readers are reminded that the gardens are private property. We are grateful to the National Gallery London, Victoria & Albert Museum, Fitzwilliam Museum, Cambridge and Wiltshire Museum, Devizes, for permission to reproduce pictures from their collections.

## Notes

1   Wordsworth C, 1917, 'Elias de Dereham's Leadenhall in Salisbury Close 1226 – 1915', in WAM 39, 433-444

2   Hastings, A, 1997, *Elias de Dereham, Architect of Salisbury Cathedral*

3   RCHM(E), 1993, *Salisbury, houses of the Close,* and Wordsworth *supra.* The house and grounds in Canon Talbot's time are shown on Naish's early to mid-18th century map of Salisbury, though on a small scale.

4   Paris L and Fleming-Williams I, 1991, *Constable*, Tate Gallery esp 224-261. Whittingham S, 1972, *Constable and Turner at Salisbury*, and Leslie CR, 1845 2nd ed, reprinted 1991, *Memoirs of the Life of John Constable.* Wilcox, T, 2011, *Constable and Salisbury, the soul of landscape.*

5   For a full biography see Cassan S H, 1824, *Lives and memoirs of the Bishops of Sherborne and Salisbury* pt 2 328-360

6   Hume was also Precentor, and acquired his position from Bishop John Hume (1766-82), Wordsworth, op cit (note 1) 443

7   See RCHM(E), 1993, op cit (note 3) 238-9

8   Surveyed in 1879. The house and garden boundary walls, before the reconstructions of c1800 are shown roughly on William Naish's 1751 map of Salisbury

9   Wordsworth op cit (note 1) 442-3. The Prince Regent came to Salisbury Races and hunted in the area.

10  Now in WANHS colllections at Wiltshire Museum. It is reproduced in RCHM(E) 1993, 236 plate 182.

11  See Mitchell A, 1996, *Trees of Britain*, 269-272

12  The stable and coach house on the north side of the yard, which runs over a medieval stone-lined water channel, was made for the Walton Canonry (No 69) to the north. All the buildings are shown on the OS 1880 map.

13  See OS 1880 plan for details.

14  The walls are mostly made with red brick basal courses and quoins, and a 'capping' of brick and tile, with a double central string-course of bricks. The rest of the wall is made of flint and reused stone.

15  A small greenhouse was first built against the north wall of the garden (at its east end) in the mid-19th century.

16  On the south side of the garden is a sundial in the form of a tilted cross.

17  Now in the Victoria and Albert Museum. No 131 in Parris and Fleming-Williams, 1991, 247. A large modern house was built on this part of the South Canonry gardens in the 1980s.

18  See Mitchell 1996 op cit, 42-5. There is a large cedar of Lebanon planted in 1803, just outside the south-east of St Alban's Abbey. Its top, however, was broken at an early date. The two cedars in the Cloister at Salisbury were planted in 1837.

19  The most recent planting of a cedar here was in 1994.

20  See Nos 132 and 133 (made in 1820) and Nos 141 and 142 in Parris and Fleming-Williams, 1991, 262. The latter two were made in July 1829 and have fine cloud effects, and the Harnham water meadows in the middle distance. Several more views that were probably made in 1820.

21  No 137 in Parris and Fleming-Williams,1991 and Wilcox, 2011, 114-122.

22  In the extreme south-west corner of the garden there is now a large horse chestnut tree. In Constable's time there was a poplar here, which is shown on the extreme right hand side of the oil painting, note 21 above. The 'great alder' and poplar can also be seen in Constable's very famour 1829 large oil painting 'Salisbury cathedral from the watermeadows' that has recently been acquired by the nation.

23  After running through a covered channel under the north side of the stable yard, the channel ran across the middle of the Marsh Closes (ie between Upper and Lower Marsh Close). It then entered the broad 'canal' in the bishop's garden, which is shown in Constable's famous view of Salisbury Cathedral from the bishop's garden. It was converted into a large pond in the mid 19th century.

24  This part of the garden can only be seen vaguely in the background of the great oil painting, note 21 above.

# Life Goes On: How Baverstock coped with the Black Death of 1348–1349

## Lucille Campey

Baverstock was one of Wilton Abbey's early possessions having been granted to the abbey by no less a figure than King Edgar, the first monarch to be recognised as King of England. Today it is a mere hamlet of Dinton; but until as recently as 1934 it was an important parish in its own right. In 968, the year when it was granted to the abbey by Edgar, Baverstock appears already to have been settled. However, in common with many other villages in the Nadder Valley, it suffered a sudden decline in its population nearly 400 years later when the Black Death of 1348–1349 struck. Nevertheless, Baverstock's community survived, although the nucleus of the village moved to a new location.

An intriguing aspect of Baverstock's medieval past is its pilgrims' rest. It was probably built to accommodate the followers of St Edith, a nun who, having died at an early age in around 984, attracted a steady stream of pilgrims to her tomb and shrine at Wilton Abbey. St Edith is linked with Baverstock both by way of being patron saint of its church[1] and by the fact that it was her father, King Edgar, who had granted it to Wilton Abbey.

Born in 961, Edith had a complicated family background. She was the product of a sexual encounter in the previous year between Edgar and Wulfthryth, a woman of noble birth who was being educated at the nunnery at Wilton Abbey. When he met her on a visit to Wilton Abbey Edgar had become so infatuated that he whisked her off to his house in Kent. The Archbishop of Canterbury later chastised Edgar for this inappropriate behaviour, but the punishment was lenient. Edgar was banned from wearing his crown for seven years. In the meantime, Wulfthryth left Kent after a year or so and returned to Wilton Abbey, taking Edith with her. Wulfthryth was then appointed abbess in accordance with Edgar's wishes and later on Edith took up her studies at the abbey.

St Edith depicted in a stained glass window in St Mary's Church, Market Place, Wilton. The glass which faces the car park was probably erected in the 19th century. Note the crown which symbolises her royal parentage and the church held in her arms which she dedicated to St Denis

Wilton was a major centre of learning at the time and as a result Edith had access to the best of teachers. According to Goscelin,[2] who wrote 'The Life of St Edith' a century after her death, she enjoyed wearing grand clothes as would befit the daughter of a king. When challenged by the Bishop of Winchester over her silks and satins Edith replied that she wore a hair-shirt under her finery. She also kept a menagerie, a kind of private zoo consisting of wild and tame animals which had been given to her as gifts.[3] Edith was both a nun and a princess. She clearly did not fit the classic stereotype of a saintly nun, but nevertheless she came to be revered as one.

According to Goscelin, Edith was offered the chance of becoming abbess at three different nunneries but in each case declined.[4] However, given that Edgar died in 975 when Edith was only about 14, these claims seem improbable. What is generally accepted is that Edith made a good impression on those around her during her short life. She devoted herself fully to religious worship and to this end had a church built in Wilton which she dedicated to St Denis, a saint to whom she had a particular devotion.[5] It was built in 984 but Edith died soon after at the tender age of twenty three. In accordance with her instructions she was buried at her church in Wilton.

Thirteen years later it was reported that Edith was appearing to people in visions, and miracles began taking place at her tomb. This led to her to being elevated to sainthood and she later became the focus of a major cult. A golden shrine was built for her at Wilton Abbey and accounts of Edith's continuing miracles attracted pilgrims over a period of around 500 years. Wilton Abbey's wealth was greatly enhanced by this influx of pilgrims but with King Henry VIII's dissolution of the monasteries in 1540, its days were numbered.[6] The abbey and St Edith's shrine were destroyed four years later.

Meanwhile, King Edgar's charter of 968, granting Baverstock to Wilton Abbey, reveals that the parish was long and thin in shape. It was bounded on the north by the Grim's Ditch in Grovely Wood, on the south by the River Nadder and on the east and west by various landmarks, which included 'the withered apple tree,' the 'red cock ditch,' 'the old meeting place fountain' and 'the street'.[7] The reference to the street (or *vicum* in the original Latin) implies a row of houses or even a village, thus making it likely Baverstock had already acquired a settled community by the time of Edgar's grant.

The next description of Baverstock is to be found in Domesday Book of 1086. The survey, undertaken for the benefit of William the Conqueror, records all lands in the country which were liable for royal taxes. Baverstock is shown as paying tax for three hides (or around 360 acres).[8] In other words it was a tiny hamlet. There was one servant (a slave) and four 'borderers', the lowest rank of serf who did not own land. Two thirds of Baverstock's land was then being run as a home farm and one third was being rented. However, while the Domesday records are of great importance, they do not provide the total population of a village. A reasonable guess is that Baverstock had a population of around 25 people in 1086.[9]

A property tax, levied by the Crown 246 years later in 1332, provides the next glimpse of Baverstock – this time of its more affluent residents. It reveals that it had seven heads of households with sufficient wealth to be liable for the tax: John Cayn, Robert in the Lane, Robert le Hert, Nicholas atte Welle, Robert Gilberde, Roger atte Hende and John atte Welle.[10] These seven householders would have each had a wife and at least three or four children and together probably accounted for around thirty five people. However, the village's many landless labourers would not have paid this tax. Undoubtedly Baverstock's population was far greater than thirty five. The first reliable head count is obtainable in 1377 when a poll tax was introduced across the country making anyone over the age of fourteen liable for the tax. It reveals that Baverstock had forty poll tax payers.[11] However, this head count took place thirty years after Baverstock's population was thought to have been decimated by the plague. While it is not possible to find statistical evidence of its population just before the Black Death of 1348–49 struck, it can reasonably be presumed that it was substantially greater than forty.

The death toll is difficult to quantify. Victims of the plague were rarely named in any part of Britain. Most villagers were illiterate, so they could not leave any documents behind. When documents relating to a village survive, they refer mainly to land owners and the religious elite.[12] However, in Baverstock's case there is a strong local tradition that lives were lost during the plague. It is believed locally that the raised church yard can be explained by the fact that a mass grave had been dug for up to 80 bodies.[13] Given that death usually occurred within three days of contracting the illness, quick burials and hastily dug mass graves were a sad reality in many parts of the country.

In a letter which he wrote to the editor of the *Salisbury Journal* in 1980 Mr J H Rideout claimed that 'in the Baverstock churchyard there is a mass grave of more then 200 people.'[14] Who was Mr Rideout? According to the South Wiltshire Poll Book, there was a William Rideout living in Baverstock in 1818 while the 1861 Census reveals a Thomas and William Rideout, both labourers and father and son born 1791 and 1830 respectively, together with William's wife Mary born 1794. Perhaps they, and others further back, were J H Rideout's ancestors who left behind information on the death toll which was passed down by various families; but that is mere speculation. Much more reliable is the archaeological evidence which confirms the presence of a deserted settlement around the church of St Edith.

The raised churchyard at Baverstock

Excavations were carried out in 1984 in an area running north/south to the east of the church.[15] Digging trenches in the right place is a hit and miss affair at the best of times and later building work added to the confusion. The site was overlain by post-medieval gardens and enclosures, a rectory which burned down in 1796, and a school and school house which were built later on the rectory site. However, archaeologists were able to confirm that the site had once accommodated a medieval settlement with Saxon origins. Further evidence of a decline in the village population during the fourteenth century comes from Archdeacon William Hony, who had been rector of Baverstock in 1827.

Archdeacon Hony responded to 'Wilkinson's Parish Questionnaire'. Having a passion for local history, the Reverend Wilkinson had persuaded the Bishop of Salisbury to send questionnaires to local parishes in 1862 asking for details about their churches. This was Archdeacon Hony's response:

> It is impossible to say what is the date of its [Baverstock's Church's] earlier portions, but there is reason to think they were Norman. When the plaster was removed from the walls a few years since, at the time when the church underwent all but a rebuilding, openings of former windows and doors were apparent in the walls; and it was the opinion of the late Mr. Rickman that a larger church had fallen into ruin, and that a small church had been built which included parts of a former church.[16]

The west end of Baverstock Church

Since Thomas Rickman was an architectural historian of great distinction, his opinion carries considerable weight. Moreover, later archaeological work proves beyond doubt that a larger church had existed on this site in the twelfth and thirteenth centuries.[17]

As is still evident today, the tower and nave at the west end of the church were built in the Perpendicular style, probably in the early 1400s. The chancel built in the Decorated style was probably present a century earlier, before the plague had struck in 1348. The timing of a new-build in the early 1400s is consistent with a village reacting to a population decline fifty or sixty years earlier. Part of Baverstock's recovery plan would have been to restore the church and reduce its size to be more in keeping with its smaller population.

Strange as it may seem, the impact of the plague on the nearby village of Hurdcott needs also to be considered. Hurdcott had been part of the ecclesiastical parish of Baverstock from ancient times. Thus, despite being some distance from Baverstock and being on the opposite side of the River Nadder, it was linked with Baverstock. Since Hurdcott had no church its dead would have been carried to Baverstock for burial – as was the case for instance, with Teffont Magna whose dead in the Middle Ages had to be buried at Dinton. Hurdcott House (the manor house) known previously as East Hurdcott, still survives; but the village known previously as West Hurdcott no longer exists.[18]

In fact Hurdcott experienced a far greater drop in its population between 1086 and 1377, than Baverstock, suggesting that the plague had reduced its population far more severely.[19] This strengthens the presumption that a significant number of bodies were buried in Baverstock at the time of the

One side of a ditch and bank enclosure to the west of the Baverstock rectory which probably accommodated sheep during the Middle Ages

## Baverstock c.1715
### Swindon and Wiltshire RO 332/284.

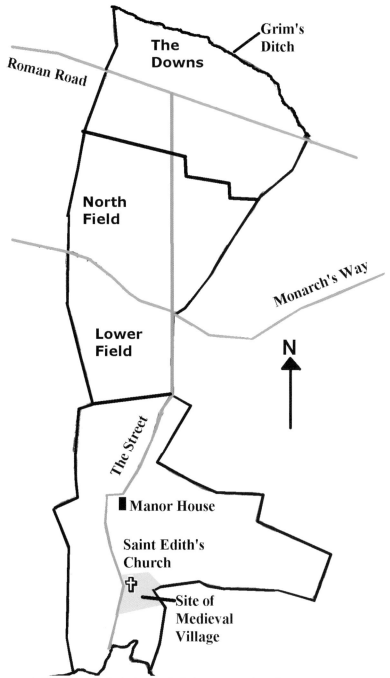

Baverstock Map c1715: Swindon & Wiltshire Record Office 332/284

Black Death. However, many would have been Hurdcott bodies. An analogy can be drawn with the thirty two World War I graves in Baverstock cemetery. The soldiers who died in the influenza outbreak of 1918–1919, had all been living in Hurdcott Camp; but they were buried in the Baverstock churchyard.[20]

Hurdcott became a deserted village but not Baverstock. Evidence on the ground and in a surviving manorial map suggests that Baverstock's survival plan involved large-scale sheep farming. One of the country's richest wool-producing counties, Wiltshire had particularly large sheep flocks, many of them owned by abbeys. They were an understandable response to the depopulation caused by the Black Death since sheep rearing was far less labour intensive than arable farming.[21] Permanent sheep houses, often timber-framed and with thatched roofs, were built to store fodder and provide shelter for at least part of the flock during bad weather. They were situated within enclosures which were often rectangular and in Wiltshire's case they were commonly called 'pennings'.[22] Surviving earthworks in the south west end of Baverstock reveal three sides of such an enclosure[23] while a c1715 map confirms the presence of a 'pennyes' and a 'penies house and pasture'.[24]

Sheep provided wool, meat and cheese and, as an added bonus, the sheep produced and deposited their own manure which added greatly to the fertility of the soil. This virtuous cycle paved the way for Baverstock's survival and steady growth. The reduced population meant that survivors of the plague had a better chance of increasing their wages. Faced with this new situation, Hurdcott labourers might have been tempted to move to Baverstock where they could get Wilton Abbey wage rates which were probably higher than the wages paid by their landlord. This could have contributed to the demise of Hurdcott.

Baverstock acquired a manor house by the sixteenth century. It was built along the village street to the north of the deserted site, this being the new centre of the village.[25]

By 1801 Baverstock's population had risen to 120 and it went on to have a golden age in the 19th century when Archdeacon Hony was Rector – a position he held for 48 years.[26] A new Rectory House was built on the opposite side of the road to the church shortly before he arrived in 1827 and during his long incumbency he organized the restoration of the church and the building of Baverstock's first school. The Powell family of Hurdcott paid for the enlargement of the Baverstock Church in the 1830s and 40 years later it experienced its second restoration under William Butterfield's supervision.[27]

Site of the former St Mary's Well in Baverstock. The walls of the manor house can be seen in the background

The manor house was close to the site of an earlier pilgrim's rest, a small two-storey house with two rooms each floor, built in 1485 by Cecilia Willoughby, Abbess of Wilton.[28] Undoubtedly the accommodation would have attracted many of Saint Edith's followers given that the then Bishop of Salisbury had granted an indulgence of 40 days to all who visited St Edith's shrine at Wilton Abbey on the anniversary of her death on16 September.[29] The house was situated close to St Mary's Well, a spring which was said to have healing properties. It was a place where visiting pilgrims bathed their eyes. Still recognisable in 1862, the well was described by Archdeacon Hony as a 'remarkable fine spring which pours forth at all times of the year providing an abundance of pure water'.[30]

Although its past is well hidden, the varied loveliness of Baverstock's landscape is very apparent today. Only fragments of medieval Baverstock's survive. The remains of a medieval cross base in the churchyard, a thirteenth century font and four flat stones with full-length crosses set in the floor either side of the alter in the church can still be seen. Few documents are available to reconstruct village life in the Middle Ages but thankfully the landscape has provided many clues.

## Illustrations

All photographs by Geoff Campey. The c1715 map is reproduced by kind permission of the Wiltshire and Swindon History Centre.

## Notes

1  The Yorkshire village of Bishop Wilton is the only other church in the country to be dedicated to St Edith of Wilton.

2  Goscelin was a Flemish monk who lived in England from c1058 until his death c1107. A hagiographer, he was a prolific writer on the lives of Anglo-Saxon saints. In his 'Legend of Edith' he made a valiant attempt to gloss over Edgar's indiscretion in carrying off Wulfthryth by referring to their marriage in c961 and claiming that it was dissolved two years later.

3  Hollis, Stephanie, 2004, 'St Edith and the Wilton Community' in Hollis and others (eds.) *Writing the Wilton Women, Goscelin's Legend of Edith and Liber confortatorius,* Turnhout, Belgium: Brepols Publishers, 245-80.

4  *ibid,* 248-9.

5  Hollis, Stephanie, 2004, 'Edith as Contemplative and Bride of Christ' in *ibid,* 292-4.

6  Journeys to holy places to obtain supernatural help or to undertake acts of penance or thanksgiving were increasingly popular in the Middle Ages. Money raised from pilgrims contributed greatly to the wealth of monasteries.

7  The grant taken from the Wilton cartulary is quoted in Colt Hoare, Sir Richard, 1829, *The Modern History of South Wiltshire,* Vol. IV, Nichols & Nichols, 96.

8  Morris, John (ed), 1979, *Domesday Book, Wiltshire,* Phillimore, 'Land of the Church of Wilton', 13-17.

9  Various scholars have suggested the use of five as a multiplier. See Darby, H C, 1986, *Domesday England,* Cambridge University Press, 87-94.

10  Crowley, D A, (ed), 1989, *The Wiltshire Tax List of 1332,* Wiltshire Record Society, 22.

11  'Poll-tax payers of 1377', in Crittall, Elizabeth, (ed), 1959, *A History of the County of Wiltshire,* Volume 4, 304-313.

12  Insights into how village life was affected by the plague are provided in Hatcher, John, 1988, *The Black Death: The Intimate Story of a Village in Crisis, 1345-1350,* Phoenix

13  For instance, during the 1940s local school children were told by their teacher that a mass grave had been dug for plague victims.

14  *Salisbury Journal,* April, 1980.

15  English Heritage National Inventory (NMR): AR70644baverstock. The medieval earthworks at Baverstock were surveyed by archaeologists from the Royal Commission of Historical Monuments in 1984. The poorly preserved remains of a small hamlet were excavated with most of the work being concentrated on the area to the east of the church.

16  The questionnaire response is quoted in Smith, W H Saumarez, 1984, *A History of Baverstock,* Spartan Press, 18.

17  *ibid,* 18-9.

18  Hurdcott is listed in 'Beresford's Lost Villages.' See www.dmv.hull.ac.uk. The grid

reference is SU 040310. Also see Beresford, Maurice and Hurst, John G, 1971, *Deserted Medieval Village Studies*, Lutterworth Press, and Beresford, Maurice, 1983, *The Lost Villages of England*, Alan Sutton

19 Hurdcott's recorded population in the Domesday Book of 1086 was 15 compared with Baverstock's population of only five. See Morris, 1979, *Domesday Book*, 'Land of Humphry De Lisle,' 27-25. In 1377 Hurdcott had 13 poll tax payers, while Baverstock had 40 tax payers.

20 The world-wide flu epidemic of 1918-1919 claimed millions of people, many of whom were servicemen. Graves of the Australian servicemen are to be found at church yards in Baverstock, Compton Chamberlayne and Fovant.

21 For a general discussion of the expansion of sheep farming after the Black Death see Dyer, Christopher, 1980, *Lords and Peasants in a Changing Society: the estates of the bishopric of Worcester, 650-1540*, University of Cambridge, 134-40. Also see Postan, M M, 1973, *Essays on Medieval Agriculture and General Problems of the Medieval Economy*, Cambridge University Press

22 The expansion of sheep farming after the Black Death in the south of England is discussed in Hare, John, 2011, *A Prospering Society: Wiltshire in the later Middle Ages*, Studies in Regional and Local History, Volume 10, University of Hertfordshire Press, 41-50. Hare provides detailed information on sheep farming on the Wiltshire estates of Winchester Cathedral Priory. A photograph of the outline of a former medieval sheep enclosure at Bishop Cannings near Devizes can be seen on page 49.

23 An aerial photograph (English Heritage D/SU0231/1) reveals a square enclosure a short distance to the west but its date and purpose is not known.

24 Wiltshire and Swindon Record Office 332/284: pen and ink map of Baverstock manor produced c1715. The 'penyes' appears on the map at the entrance to a lane leading to the field containing the enclosure while the 'penies house' appears at the south west end of the parish.

25 Baverstock manor house is a Grade II listed building of the sixteenth and seventieth centuries. It was restored in the 1930s.

26 For details of Archdeacon Hony's time in Baverstock see Gandy, Ida, 1963, *Staying with the Aunts*, Harvill Press

27 Smith, *History of Baverstock*, 41-53.

28 *ibid*, 22.

29 'Houses of Benedictine nuns: Abbey of Wilton', in Pugh, R B, and Crittall, Elizabeth (eds), 1956, *A History of the County of Wiltshire*: Volume 3 London, 231-242. The indulgence, granted in 1425, offered pilgrims the hope of spending 40 fewer days in Purgatory.

30 Smith, *History of Baverstock*, 22.

# Veterinary Surgeons of Salisbury

## Sam Cutler

### Background

The science that we now call veterinary medicine can be traced back to *c*3000 BC. The first veterinary college in the UK was established in 1791—The London Veterinary College (LVC), which later became The Royal Veterinary College (RVC). The opening of the LVC and its associated formal veterinary qualification founded the veterinary profession in the UK. The title 'Veterinary Surgeon' was first used by Army Officers in 1796 and is believed to have been derived from the Roman 'veterinarium', which was a hospital for sick and wounded horses. In 1823 the second UK college was founded by The Highland Society's Veterinary School in Edinburgh and was later to become the Dick Vet. Following on from this the Veterinary Medical Association held its first meeting in 1836 and a Royal Charter created The Royal College of Veterinary Surgeons (RCVS) in 1844.

Unfortunately for the newly developing profession, the courses offered by these colleges were at first very short and superficial and did little to distinguish the newly qualified men from the existing experienced, but unqualified, practitioners. At the end of the 18th century many of the unqualified practitioners were farriers and they were usually literate individuals represented by the Company of Farriers. Less well-educated 'practitioners' were known by various local appellations such as horse-doctors, horse-surgeons, blacksmiths, cow-leeches, cattle doctors, castrators, spayers, gelders, charmers, spell-workers, butty-colliers and water-doctors. They had knowledge and experience of animal illness and commonly used their own remedies from family receipt books, almanacs, or popular husbandry books, as well as remedies purchased from pharmacists, medicine

Hand Cranked Veterinary Centrifuge c1930s (Photography by Roy Bexon)

vendors and specialist 'veterinary chemists'. Many livestock owners, grooms, coachmen, shepherds and cowmen did not immediately accept the newly qualified veterinary surgeon or even seek the help of an unqualified practitioner, especially if a cure seemed unlikely, as they could cut their losses by butchering or selling the animal rather than spend money employing someone else to help.

Commonly the men who did attend college were the sons of farmers, farriers or smiths, but not all of those who attended the colleges completed their studies or passed their final exams, possibly reflecting the fact that they were less educated. In addition many unqualified men started to use the title Veterinary Surgeon. This may have been an attempt to confer some sort of market advantage to their businesses.

As the number of qualified men grew during the 19th Century the RCVS (in order to distinguish the new class of scientifically trained individuals qualifying from these establishments) attempted in 1866 to establish a monopoly on the use of the title 'Veterinary Surgeon' and proposed that qualified men (women were not allowed to attend college) and unqualified practitioners who had been 'in practice' prior to 1844 were the only people who could exclusively call themselves Veterinary Surgeons. This was not granted at this time. However, as the training gradually became better and a clearer distinction between untrained veterinary practitioners and formally trained and examined veterinary surgeons emerged, the Veterinary Surgeons Act was passed in 1881 and the title 'Veterinary Surgeon' became exclusive, finally enabling a distinction between the new class of scientifically trained diploma holders from farriers and others.

Various terms were used to describe the emerging businesses of the early veterinary surgeons. The keeping of a 'veterinary infirmary' was an establishment in which sick horses were stabled, whereas a 'veterinary forge' was where healthy ones were shod. Many qualified veterinary surgeons in the mid-19th century also sold services of farriery, forge or horse-shoeing alongside their professional services. In general these additional activities were performed by farriers or smiths employed by the veterinary owner of the establishment. They also pursued other horse-related lines of work such as stabling, livery or horse hire. Many also had connections with public houses on the basis that carters and coaches would stop there—often performing the dual function of publican and veterinarian.

When the LVC opened in 1791 Salisbury was a fair sized market town with a population of just over 7,500 which was only approximately 9,500 by 1851. However, by the start of the 20th century the population had grown more rapidly, reaching 17,000 by 1901. Until the arrival of the railways in Salisbury in 1847 the main mode of transport was by horse and coach and so horse health was vitally important. As Salisbury was a hub for travel it provided a number of busy thoroughfares for the veterinary surgeons to choose for setting up their businesses.

## Early to Mid 19th Century Veterinary Surgeons

The earliest person from Salisbury to have attended the LVC was Lewis Osmond Weeks. He qualified on 25th March 1808[1], aged 28 years, and advertised in the Salisbury Journal in May of the same year that he intended to establish a Veterinary Forge in Brown Street.[2] It is not clear exactly where the site of his Brown Street Veterinary Forge was located but it may have been where the house at 83 Brown Street is situated today as we know that the current building was built on the site of two cottages owned by the Weeks family.[3] This site would have been an ideal location as it is almost opposite what is today the rear entrance of The White Hart and so would have been very convenient for treating the horses stabled there and for treating those that pulled the coaches for The White Hart Coach Company. The White Hart Coach Company was a family business established in 1772 by William Weeks, father of Lewis. William was also proprietor of the White Hart Inn from 1772–1798.[4] By 1809 The White Hart Coach Company had become known as Weeks's Coach Offices and these were advertised as being located "opposite the White Hart Inn" so it would seem likely that 83 Brown Street was indeed the location of the first 'veterinary' business in Salisbury.[5]

The Weeks family were also the owners of one or more of the horses pulling the Quicksilver Exeter To London Mail Coach which was famously attacked by a lioness on the night of 20th October 1816.[6] Presumably Lewis was the veterinary surgeon who treated the injured horse, Pomegranate. This horse recovered from its wounds but bore the scars and was exhibited by Ballard, the owner of the lioness, in his travelling menagerie the following year.

Both William and Lewis were members of the Wiltshire Yeoman Cavalry and Lewis in particular appears to have been an accomplished rider and competed at various times on different horses in the Yeoman's Cup.[7]

The family were also, alongside the Arundell and Peniston households, one of the prominent Catholic families of Salisbury, and in 1844[8] when there was a prestigious visit from King of Saxony it was Lewis who had the honour of escorting him through the City following a service at the Roman Catholic Chapel.[9]

In 1842 Lewis relocated the coach business, and possibly his veterinary business, to Catherine Street.[10] It is unclear why he did this and it is equally unclear what happened to the veterinary side of Lewis's business when he died in 1855 aged 75 years. By this time his son, originally a farmer at Clarendon Park,[11] had moved to London and there is no trace of a sale of the business to another veterinary surgeon. His widow left Salisbury in 1860 – advertising the premises in Brown Street for rent and selling the furniture at auction.[12] Most likely his business was absorbed by a young veterinary surgeon named Thomas Aubrey also working from Brown Street.

Another prominent veterinary surgeon of the early 19th century was Joseph Snow and he ran his premises from just around the corner from Lewis. Joseph was the son of James Snow, a stud owner from Sixpenny Handley. Joseph entered veterinary college in 1833 and qualified from the LVC on 1st May 1834, starting his business almost immediately afterwards.[13] He based himself in St John Street and so very close to the Weeks at the

White Hart & Brown Street. In fact Joseph even went as far as advertising his business as being 'near The White Hart Inn.'[14] How this went down with his business rival is unclear! There may well have been intense rivalry as in 1834 a rumour was spread, via delivery of cards, that Lewis was going to relinquish his practice and it may be that the entrepreneurial Joseph, wanting to gain clients, was the source of this rumour. Lewis had to counter this rumour by placing an advertisement to say it was untrue.[15] Whatever the situation, Joseph and his business seemed to prosper even though at one point in 1840 he succumbed to illness for a period and had to employ an assistant.[16] This was probably because he had contracted TB from which he later died in 1855.

Joseph Snow was an early advocate of the use of chloroform for anaesthesia in horses. The use of chloroform was in its infancy having only being used for the first time in 1847 by Simpson in the human field and Flourens in the veterinary field. Joseph used chloroform to render a horse insensible using apparatus provided by a chemist named Whitlock, and carried out an operation to divide a nerve in the animal's foot. Joseph also chose to administer the chloroform before the horse was cast to show that it was the chloroform that rendered the horse insensible and not the procedure of casting as some believed.[17] This was a very advanced technique as the use of chloroform did not become widespread until 1853, after it was administered to Queen Victoria by Dr John Snow during the birth of her eighth child. Although it seems to be too much of a co-incidence to have two men involved in the early days of chloroform anaesthesia named Snow, to my knowledge there is no link between them.

In 1856, just one year after his death, Joseph's widow sold his veterinary business to Thomas Aubrey.[18]

But what of the unqualified men? Did they practice in Salisbury? There is evidence to show that there was at least one such practitioner of note working in Salisbury in the first half of the 19th century – a Mr James Kite.

James first appears on the veterinary scene in Salisbury in 1819 having possibly been practising in Hindon for four years prior to that. In addition to practising as a veterinary surgeon (he advertised himself as a member of the RCVS) he was the proprietor of a number of public establishments. In September 1829 he advertised that he was relinquishing his 'Public Line of Business' (at The Roebuck, Canal Street) to 'devote himself to his (veterinary) profession entirely' and moved to 'more commodious' premises near The Dolphin Inn on Culver Street.[19] This move may have been precipitated by an increased demand on his veterinary skills following countrywide newspaper coverage in June that year when he extracted the eye of a horse and with it a tumour weighing $16^{1/}_{4}$ oz – he preserved the eye in spirits 'for the curious to observe.'[20] However it appears that he did not stick to this plan entirely as there is evidence to show that he continued to be involved as a Publican at various locations including The Butchers Arms in Market Street in 1832 and The Wheatsheaf Inn on New Canal in 1834 before finally ending up at The Bell Inn on Milford Hill from 1836–1844.[21] He was the first veterinary surgeon in Salisbury to advertise services for dogs as well as horses. James seemed to be quite happy to promote himself as a veterinary surgeon rather than a practitioner. His daybook for 1842–5 has survived and gives us an insight into the type of clients and services he was able to provide.[22] At this time he had 125 clients, many located in Fovant, Dinton and Tisbury and they included the Marquis of Westminster.

James died in November 1846 from gout and gastroenteritis.[23] It is unclear what then happened to his business as his son had moved to London and although one of his daughters married another veterinary surgeon this gentleman did not practise his profession in Salisbury. There is nothing in the Salisbury Journal advertising the sale of his business either. His clients would have been left seeking the services of Lewis Weeks or Joseph Snow.

As well as being a Publican and Veterinary Surgeon we know that James also owned and rented land around Salisbury and kept cattle. When he became ill in 1844 it appears that he could no longer manage his cattle and land as he advertised one acre of meadow land near the bridge in Laverstock for sale and a six cow dairy, milk walk and one or two meadows if required.[24]

**Mid to Late 19th Century Veterinary Surgeons**

Thomas Aubrey, the son of a farrier, trained at the LVC and qualified in May 1854 when he was 22 years old.[25] Thomas started his veterinary career working from the premises of the Black Horse Inn in Brown Street.[26] This location provides a link between Thomas and Lewis Weeks – Thomas started his veterinary career at The Black Horse Inn and Lewis was an owner of The Black Horse Coach Company that departed from The Black Horse Inn. Moreover, another of Lewis's coaches ran from The Lamb Inn in Catherine Street and in 1859 Thomas bought The Lamb Inn and moved his veterinary business there.[27] These tantalising snippets of information perhaps mean nothing more than the properties were just both conducive to running a veterinary business. However it is clear that Thomas's practice appears as to have become the main veterinary business in the Brown Street/Catherine Street locality from 1856 as a result of establishing his own business and also probably taking on Lewis's business when Lewis died in 1855. Either he legitimately purchased it or was by default the only other veterinary

Ether     Vaporizer     c1920s
(Photography by Roy Bexon)

surgeon in the immediate locality. He also bought the practice of Joseph Snow in 1856[28] – one year after the death of Joseph who also died in 1855,[29] and then in 1857 went on to buy the veterinary business of the late Daniel Tabor which was based in Quidhampton and had been run by veterinary practitioner Robert Cusse following the death of Daniel.[30]

Thomas continued to prosper and by 1871 he had moved his business from the site of The Lamb Inn at 45 Catherine Street to 16–18 Catherine Street. Deeds for these premises give us an insight into what was required to run a successful veterinary practice as at number 16 he had a '3 floor premises with numerous outbuildings – on the ground floor he had 2 sitting rooms with an office behind, a kitchen and surgery over the same; 5 bedrooms on the first floor and 3 offices on the second floor. There was a stable yard with 4 stall stables and a loft over, a saddle room, 7 loose boxes with a loft over and 2 further loose boxes plus a coach house adjoining.'[31]

Thomas was not the sole practitioner at this time as a number of other

Signature and seal of Thomas Aubrey (Photography by Sam Cutler)

veterinary surgeons practised in Salisbury around the middle of the 19th century but apparently only for a few years. John Coleman from Tilshead, who qualified from the LVC in May 1847, was the most notable of these. He started his career in Tilshead, probably working for his father who was also an unqualified veterinary practitioner.[32] John seemed to be concerned particularly with livestock rather than horses and he regularly advertised medicines such as condition balls and chill drenches and the 'Coleman's Celebrated Tenting for Wounds.'[33] It is not clear if the latter was a family recipe or a product for treating ailments endorsed by Professor Edward Coleman, second principal of the LVC from 1793 to 1839.

The remaining veterinary surgeons were of minor note and were either employed by the more prominent practitioners or their businesses failed.[34]

## Late 19th Century Veterinary Surgeons

In the second half of the 19th century Joseph Charles Truckle set up business in Bridge Street on the other side of the city to Thomas Aubrey. Joseph was originally from Fordingbridge but moved to Salisbury when his father took up the position of Head Dairyman at Bemerton Dairy. Joseph was apprenticed to Daniel Tabor of Quidhampton.[35] He qualified in 1853 from the LVC only six months before Thomas Aubrey.[36]

In February 1854, just two months after qualifying, Joseph advertised that he intended to set up his business in Bridge Street, next door to the London Inn.[37] By 1860 he was in Fisherton Street 'opposite The Bull Inn.'[38] Later the same year he bought a shoeing business that had been established for 25 years from Owen Perman a farrier.[39] In 1861 he went on to buy the veterinary business of George Henry Morton.[40] This was very similar to what Thomas was doing and both went on to become prominent veterinary surgeons in Salisbury during the latter half of the 19th century, holding many important local posts.[41]

As we know Thomas initially worked from the premises of the late Black Horse Inn on the corner of Brown Street and Winchester Street. In 1859 these premises were let and Thomas relocated to The Lamb Inn at 45 Catherine Street having acquired the practices of Joseph Snow and Robert Cusse in the intervening years.

During the Cattle Plague outbreaks in 1869 Thomas received a glowing affidavit from the Marquis of Bath who commented that 'Mr Aubrey, was, perhaps, certainly one of the best veterinary inspectors not only in the southern division, but anywhere, and therefore they could not have a better man than him' and 'stood as high as anybody could stand in the South of England, and he did not think they could do better.'[42]

On October 27th 1891 Thomas let his premises in Catherine Street to Scottish Veterinary Surgeon George Parr and relocated to Bath to work with his father-in-law who was also a veterinary surgeon but nearing retirement.[43] Thomas became an FRCVS by examination in 1893.[44]

## Late 19th to Early 20th Century Veterinary Surgeons

Ernest Harding qualified from the RVC on 1st April 1880 moving to Salisbury in 1885 to work with his Uncle, Joseph Truckle. He practised at 40 Fisherton Street before relocating to 39 Castle Street sometime before 1928 and retired in 1936.

Ernest died in 1948 and according to his obituary he was held in high regard by farmers and other clients for his skill and devotion to his work, was a Veterinary Inspector for the city of Salisbury and on many occasions called to give professional evidence in magistrate's courts.[45]

George Parr bought the Catherine Street Practice of Thomas Aubrey in 1893. George was the first Veterinary Surgeon to work in Salisbury who had studied and qualified at the Dick Vet School in Edinburgh. The son of a farmer from Midlothian, he was Scottish by birth and started his career in Shifnal, Shropshire. He moved to Salisbury to work for Thomas Aubrey, eventually buying the business and establishing himself as the main competitor to Ernest Harding. After ten years George relocated from Catherine Street to bigger premises in Endless Street, purchasing Number 47 in 1901.[46] He held various official posts and he was one of the first veterinary surgeons to have used a motor-car for his work.[47]

In 1923 George Parr applied for planning permission to build a house

Lease Surrender Thomas Aubrey to George Parr 1891 (Photography by Sam Cutler)

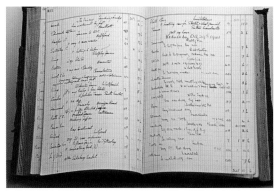

1941 Daybook entries (Photography by Roy Bexon)

at 49 Endless Street.[48] George retired the following year and the Salisbury Telephone Directory for 1925 confirms H.C. Rockett as 'Veterinary Surgeon, 49 Endless Street' so we know that Herbert Rockett succeeded George Parr. The house at 49 was not completed as a private residence until 1926 when the deeds of conveyance show transfer of ownership from George Parr to Herbert Rockett.[48] After this time the stables at 49 were used as the business premises with the house being the senior partners' private accommodation.[50]

Herbert Charles Rockett was from Devon and entered the RVC in 1910 qualifying in 1915.[51] He then joined the Army Veterinary Corps (which

JB White (Image courtesy of RCVS Knowledge)

became the Royal Army Veterinary Corps in 1918). He was promoted to Major and awarded an OBE.[52] He left in 1919 and joined George Parr in Endless Street sometime between 1919 and 1924.[53]

Herbert Rockett had an unusual business relationship with Ernest Harding in that they employed a shared veterinary assistant. This was John Beveridge (also known as JB or Jack) White.[54] JB qualified from the RVC on 13 July 1927.[55]

JB White and another RAVC veterinary surgeon, Major Wallace, later became partners with Rockett and the business became known as 'Rockett, White and Wallace' by 1939.[56]

## Mid 20th Century Veterinary Surgeons

Rockett retired in 1946[57] and John 'Jack' Beveridge White took over the helm of senior partner. The son of a veterinary surgeon from Petersfield, he was a member of the RCVS Council between 1953 and 1967 serving as President, Vice-President and Treasurer. He was also President of the British Veterinary Association from 1962–63 and was elected FRVCS in 1968. On his retirement from UK practice, in 1967, he emigrated to Australia to be near his son, but continued working as a veterinary surgeon in Australia until full retirement.[58]

Major Wallace at work (Image courtesy of Ian Wallace)

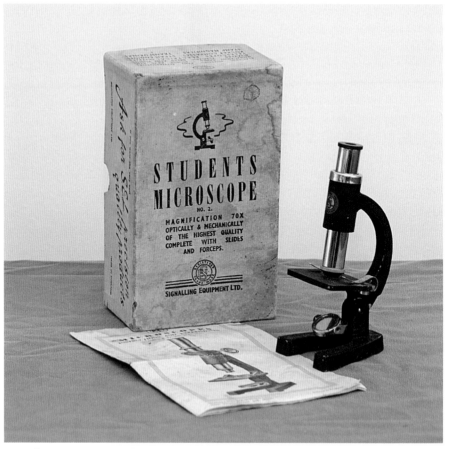

Signalling Equipment Ltd Student's Microscope c1940–50s (Photography by Roy Bexon)

Major Eric Wallace, who joined the practice at Endless Street sometime between 1932 and 1937, became the next senior partner. After Wallace qualified he joined the RAVC and he spent most of his army years in India but had been stationed at Bulford Camp on Salisbury Plain at one point. His son believes that he may have been drawn back to work in Salisbury because he liked what he had seen of the area during his time at Bulford Camp. Wallace was well liked and respected by equine clients as he was a good rider himself and understood horses.[59]

In 1972, just a few years after JB retired, Eric Wallace also retired and the business became then became known as Pook & Partners.

Harold 'Harry' Lucas Pook had graduated from the Dick Vet on 18th July 1941 and served with the RAVC until at least 1948 reaching the rank of Captain. He worked at Endless Street between 1950 and 1978 becoming senior Partner in 1972. He died in January 1996.[60]

After Pook retired in 1978 the business took on the name of Grater & Partners. George Grater qualified from the RVC in 1944 and also spent time in the RAVC. Pook and Grater are both names that are still widely recognised today particularly within the local farming community.

In 1986 George Grater retired and the new senior partner, Gerry Humphreys, proposed a radical idea that rather than change the title of the business every few years it would be sensible to use a name that was not related to the current senior partner. The name Endell Veterinary Group was chosen, and has remained that ever since. Between 1901 and 1986 the business operated at various times out of the house at 47 and the house at 49, before finally ending up at number 49 Endless Street.[61] Endell Veterinary Group is therefore the oldest veterinary practice in Salisbury. There are now a number of others in the city but all except one are modern. None of them other than Endell Veterinary Group has roots that can be traced back more than 200 years, nor can claim to have witnessed the transition from unqualified practitioner to professionally-qualified veterinary surgeon.

## Bibliography

Dorling, E.E, 1906, *Wilts and Dorset at the opening of the twentieth century. Contemporary biographies*, Pike, W.T, Brighton

Pattison, Iain, 1984, *The British Veterinary Profession 1791–1948,* J.A. Allen & Company Ltd London

Vivash-Jones, Bruse, Global Veterinary Timeline **www.knowledge.rcvs.org.uk** (accessed March 2015)

Woods, A & Matthews, S,2010, 'Little, if at all, Removed from the Illiterate Farrier or Cow-Leech'. The English Veterinary Surgeon, c.1860–1885, and the Campaign for Veterinary Reform, *Med Hist* 54(1), 24–54

## Abbreviations

*EVG = Endell Veterinary Group Ltd*
*RCVS = The Royal College of Veterinary Surgeons*
*RVC = the Royal Veterinary College*
*SJ = The Salisbury and Winchester Journal*
*VR = The Veterinary Record*
*WRS = Wiltshire Record Society*
*WSA = Wiltshire and Swindon Archives*
*WSRO = Wiltshire and Swindon Record Office*
*WYC = Wiltshire Yeoman Cavalry*

## Notes

1.  Personal Communication from RVC Registers by RVC Archivist

2. SJ 6 June 1808 1 & 25 May 1809 4
3. Howells, J & Newman, R, 2011 (eds) *William Small's Cherished Memories and Associations* WRS 53
4. SJ 12 Dec 1772 1
5. SJ 19 Jun 1809 1
6. SJ 08 September 1817 3
7. Chester Courant of 26 Aug 1800 1 Lewis, of the Salisbury Troop, competes on horse Tactic in the Yeomanry Cup; SJ 27 Aug 1810 4 there is a reference to William Weeks being a cornet in the Regiment; SJ 11 Aug 1807 2 Lewis entered with bay mare 'Catalani' in the Cavalry Cup at Salisbury Races. This was a race for 'horses belonging to the regiment to be rode by Yeoman'; SJ Oct 27 1817 4 Lewis is appointed Veterinary Surgeon to WYC (Wiltshire Regiment)
8. Crittall, Elizabeth, 1962 *'Salisbury: Roman Catholicism', in A History of the County of Wiltshire'* 6 155–156 London via http://www.britishhistory.ac.uk/vch/wilts/vol6/pp155–156 (accessed March 2015)
9. Wiltshire Independent Thursday 11 July 1844 3
10. SJ 10 December 1842 4
11. SJ 12 July 1851 2
12. SJ 6 Oct 1860 4 and 13 Oct 1860 4
13. Personal Communication from RVC Registers by RVC Archivist
14. SJ 6 Oct 1834 4
15. SJ 27 Oct 1834 4 and 3 Nov 1834 4
16. SJ 16 Nov 1840 4
17. SJ 25 Mar 1848 4
18. SJ 19 Apr 1856 2
19. SJ 21 Sep 1829 4
20. In June 1829 various newspapers around the country reported the 'wonderful operation' performed by James Kite
21. SJ 14 Nov 1836 4
22. WSRO 776/930, James Kite, account book
23. 1845 James Kite Death Certificate FHL 1279404 Ref ID 1279404
24. SJ 29 Jun 1844 4
25. SJ 20 May 1854 3; RVC Archives show he entered the college on 19 October 1852 and gave his previous occupation as 'practitioner' so he may have been working as an unqualified veterinary surgeon alongside his farrier father or may have been working for either Lewis Weeks or Joseph Snow. The 1851 England Census TNA HO 107/1847 f220 27 lists him as an apprentice Smith.
26. SJ 15 Jul 1843 4
27. SJ 24 Dec 1859 4
28. SJ 19 April 1856 2
29. SJ 4 Aug 1855 3
30. SJ 30 May 1857 2
31. WSRO 1029/1
32. SJ 8 May 1847 4
33. SJ 1861 23 Feb 5 Advert for Coleman's celebrated tenting wounds
34. There are many references to the minor veterinary surgeons who worked in

Salisbury the period 1835 to 1875. Examples of these are 1841 England Census TNA HO 107/1190/7 Jake Delainey; SJ 28 October 1854 2 Robert Cusse & Daniel Tabor; SJ 2 May 1857 2 George Henry Morton; Post Office Directory of Hampshire, Isle of Wight, Wiltshire & Dorset 1875 743 George Folliott Young; SJ 1Apr 1865 4; SJ 1 Oct 1867 4; SJ 29 Jun 1872 5 John Coleman Junior; SJ 4 May 1835 1 Robert & John Coleman

35. SJ 7 October 1854 2

36. SJ 24 December 1853 4

37. SJ 7 October 1854 2

38. SJ 14 January 1860 4

39. SJ 24 November 1860 5

40. SJ 19 January 1861 4 George Henry Morton was a Salisbury based VS who sold his business and moved to Australia to become a teacher. He advertised his business on a 'No cure, no pay' basis so this may have been the reason for the failure!

41. SJ 08 Feb 1868 4

42. SJ 23 Oct 1869 6; The Cattle Plague Epidemic of 1865–6 was in effect the start of Animal Health legislation to protect the UK from imported diseases

43. Private Deeds of EVG Ltd

44. The Bath Chronicle & Weekly 02 Feb 1893 8

45. VR, June 19 1948, 60(25), 308

46. Private Deeds of EVG

47. https://salisburyinquests.wordpress.com/ (accessed March 2015); *Sidney Mitchell 1915 January 22 knocked down by a car*

48. WSA 1923 771 G23/760/231

49. Private Deeds of EVG

50. Personal communication with Norman Comben MRCVS

51. Personal communication with RVC Archivist

52. Supplement to the London Gazette, 27 August, 1919 10834

53. Personal communication with RVC Archivist

54. VR, June 5 1965, 77(23) 650

55. Personal Communication from RCVS Library

56. Private Documents of EVG

57. Personal Communication from RCVS Library

58. VR, September 9 1989 307

59. Personal communication with Ian Wallace son of Major Eric Wallace

60. VR, January 20 1996, 70

61. Personal communications with Suzie Dalboozi, Gerry Humphreys, Nigel Richards, Ian Wallace and Lynne Worwood

Fig. 1 Detail of the Milford tithe award. Milford Hill is at the top with Fowler's Hill and Southampton Rd at the bottom. Icehouses were recorded in plots 248, 249 and 293

# Three Icehouses and a Rackhouse in Milford

## Jamie Wright

After the restoration of the Monarchy in 1660 icehouses became fashionable almost overnight, but only the wealthy could afford them. Through the 18th century more icehouses were built, initially by wealthy landowners and farmers, but by the end of the century they were becoming common in urban centres. Three icehouses are recorded in Milford on the 1844 tithe award, two at the top of Milford Hill and one near Southampton Road (Fig. 1, **248**, **249** and **293**).[1] Later maps show the area in more detail and the Salisbury drainage map of 1854, drawn at a scale of 1:500, shows two green shaded enclosures, without internal features, to the south of Milford Hill while the enclosure to the south of Southampton Road is shown, within which is a small circular structure. To the south of Milford Hill, the Ordnance Survey (OS), 1:500 map of 1880, surveyed in 1879, shows two enclosures each containing a mound, defined by hachures, and each with a wall at the northern end (Fig 2). On Southampton Road the structure, present on the 1854 map, is mapped (Fig. 3).

Icehouses were built in a wide variety of shapes, sizes and materials.[2] The earliest ones were an inverted cone shape, and in the 18th century they changed to the egg shape associated with country houses. By the 19th century many design innovations were introduced leading to square, rectangular and tunnel-shaped forms and, increasingly, built above ground level. Good drainage was one of the most important factors for the preservation of ice, as wet ice melts quickly,[3] this may explain why no icehouses are known to have been built in central Salisbury. Icehouses were frequently built on a slope or next to a ditch to allow water to run off from a drain in the base of the structure.

The two examples on Milford Hill are both at least partially above ground,

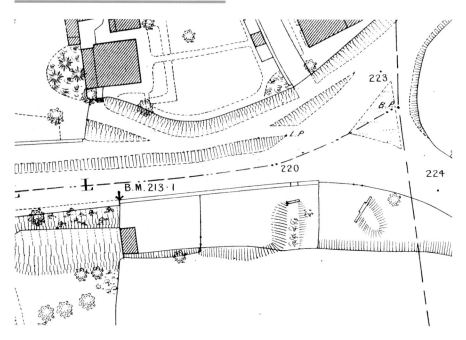

*Above*: Fig. 2 Detail showing the two icehouses to the southwest of the junction of Milford Hill, Laverstock Rd and Shady Bower. OS 1:500 map of 1880, surveyed 1879, Sheet LXVI, 15.5

*Right*: Fig. 3 Detail showing Southampton Rd and St Martin's church with the circular icehouse to the right of the saw pit. OS 1:500 map of 1880, surveyed 1879, Sheet LXVI, 15.10

possibly with the material that formed the insulating mound having been excavated to create space underground. Both of these icehouses had walls at their northern end where a door would have given access to the interior. As shown on the 1880 OS map, the top of the mound of the western icehouse on Milford Hill measured *c*7.5m by 2m and the eastern mound was smaller at *c*4m by 2m. The smaller size of the eastern mound could suggest that this icehouse was the earlier of the two. Also on the 1880 OS map the Southampton Road icehouse had a diameter of 5m, with a 2.5m by 2m conjoined rectangle forming the entrance, the dimensions shown on the Drainage map were slightly smaller. No mound is shown for this icehouse and it may have been subterranean.

The archive of the Church Commissioners (CC, the successors to the Ecclesiastical Commission), held by the Wiltshire and Swindon Archives (WSA), also refers to the icehouses on Milford Hill and gives some of the lessees.[4] J Simmonds held the lease in 1828 and may have been Rev. J.

Simmonds of Hog Lane.[5] The next lessees listed by the CC were Isaac White and John Fielder, who held the properties in 1838, the first time that there were concurrent entries. John Fielder still held the lease in 1844, when the tithe award was prepared, but Isaac White had been replaced by John White.[6]

Isaac White of Catherine St and John Fielder of Milford St were both confectioners.[7] No record of John White has been found but it is probable that he was a relative of Isaac, who was recorded as a baker in the 1790s, and had presumably stopped trading 50 years later.[8] Some details about Fielder's business are revealed in the *Salisbury and Winchester Journal* (SJ). An advertisement of 1848 announced 'Refreshment Saloons, Milford Street, Salisbury: J. Fielder, cook and confectioner, begs most respectfully to inform the Nobility, Clergy, Gentry and the Public at large, that he has opened the above saloons'.[9] Among the foods offered for sale were ices, jellies, creams etc; ice was used to set jellies and aspics, and to freeze cream and fruit ices.[10] Fielder had been a confectioner since at least 1835 as the advertisement hoped that the patronage and support that he had previously received would

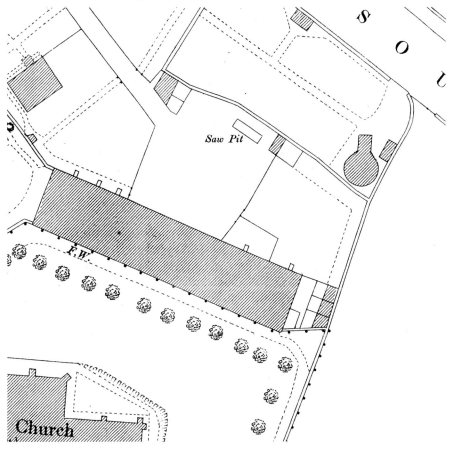

be continued, while a later advertisement, from 1865, was for 'Confectionary and refreshment rooms, established 1835. H Ward (late Fielder and Son) cook, pastrycook, and confectioner, Milford Street, Salisbury'; this also offered ices, jellies, creams etc.[11]

At least one icehouse was still in use in 1872, as Messrs Ewen & Winstanley had received instructions to sell by auction various properties, including a 'leasehold icehouse, situate on Milford Hill, and now in the occupation of Mrs Brown'.[12] The lot was held by lease under the Ecclesiastical Commissioners for a term of 99 years, determinable with the life of a lady aged 50 years or thereabouts.

The icehouse on Southampton Road was leased to Edward Baker and Charles Farr in 1844 and no other lessees are recorded. Col Edward Baker of St Ann St was listed under the heading Nobility, Gentry and Clergy, and Charles Farr & Son of Catherine St were coach builders.[13] It seems probable that they, and Rev J Simmonds on Milford Hill, had the icehouses for domestic use. As well as setting jellies and aspics, and freezing cream and fruit ices, ice was used to cool champagne and punch. In America in the middle of the 19th century ice boxes or refrigerators were common,[14] and were probably used in Britain by those with access to a constant supply of ice. Ice was an important household item and Hart's former butcher's shop, established between 1880 and 1885 in Butcher Row,[15] still announces to the Market Square that fish, game, poultry and ice were for sale.

When the icehouses went out of use is unknown. Ice-making machines are known from 1858 and 1862 but they were large and were only slowly adopted.[16] Norwegian ice was still being imported to Southampton in 1889, for distribution by train, and G Thomas, ice merchant, was advertising at the Royal Pier station, Southampton in 1900.[17] Mapped by the OS in 1901 at 1:2500 the enclosures on Milford Hill and Southampton Road still existed but no internal structures were shown, the enclosures were partially delineated in 1925 and had disappeared by 1937. Generally, the First World War saw the decline of icehouses due to the unavailability of staff to maintain them.

The story of the Milford Hill icehouses is not quite finished though, as the CC archive refers to 'the rackhouse or icehouse tenement'.[18] The first three lessees of this tenement, A Courtney (in 1784), Joseph Everett (in 1895) and J Sutton (in 1810) were all involved in the cloth trade. Bailey's trade directory lists Ambrose Courtney and Joseph Everett simply as manufacturers, but a slightly later directory gives Courtney & Co and Everett & Co as clothiers.[19] James Sutton of Milford Street was a clothier while John Sutton was co-owner of West Harnham fulling mill, and the fulling mill at Milford was leased between 1786 and 1830 to members of the Sutton family.[20]

No references to the use of a rackhouse in the woollen industry have been found, and it is not clear for what it was used, nor what the meaning of rack is in this context: it seems to be an idiomatic use. After fulling the cloth was racked to dry, to gain an even bleach and if necessary to stretch it. Cloth drying racks (tenterhook racks) are depicted on the eastern slope of Milford Hill on a panoramic painting of Salisbury,[21] and on Andrews and Dury's map are shown, by fence-like symbols, covering much of Milford Hill. It is unlikely that cloth was being dried inside what would have been a relatively small building and it is possible that dried cloth was temporarily stored in the rackhouse. The dates that the rackhouse is known to have been used, between 1784 and 1828 or possibly 1838, are those of the final decline of the clothing industry in Salisbury, where 24 clothiers in 1798 were reduced to 13 by 1814, with only three in 1830 and apparently none by 1843.[22] Presumably the rackhouse was no longer economically rewarding and it was replaced or rebuilt as an icehouse, with a second one built later.

## Acknowledgements

I am grateful to the Wiltshire and Swindon Archives, particularly Claire Skinner, and the Salisbury branch of Wiltshire Library, especially Darren Wells, for their help and courtesy. Wiltshire and Swindon Archives are also thanked for permission to reproduce the Milford tithe award. Hannah Lyddy of Trowbridge Museum replied promptly to an inquiry about rackhouses and is thanked for her help. Pat Shelley has commented on a draft of this article trying to make it a more interesting read, his help is appreciated and any failings are the author's.

## References

Bailey, 1783, *Western & Midland Directory*, Birmingham, Pearson & Rollason

Beamon, S P and Roaf, S, 1990, *The Ice-Houses of Britain*, Routledge

Chandler, John, 1983, *Endless Street; A History of Salisbury and its People*, Hobnob Press

David, Elizabeth, 1996, *Harvest of the Cold Months: The Social History of Ice and Ices*, Penguin

Ellis, M, 1982, *Ice and Icehouses through the Ages; With a Gazetteer for Hampshire*, Southampton University Industrial Archaeology Group

Kelly, 1880, *Directory of Hampshire, with the Isle of Wight, Wiltshire and Dorsetshire*, Kelly

Kelly, 1885, *Directory of Wiltshire, Dorsetshire and Hampshire*, Kelly

Pigot, 1822, *London and Provincial New Commercial Directory*, Pigot

Pigot, 1830, *London and Provincial New Commercial Directory*, Pigot

Pigot, 1842, *London and Provincial New Commercial Directory*, Pigot

Rogers, Kenneth H, 1976, *Wiltshire and Somerset Woollen Mills*, Pasold Research Fund

Slater, 1850, *Royal National and Commercial Directory*

Tatton-Brown, Tim, with Howells, Jane, 2014, 'A later 18th century painting of Salisbury from the south-west', *Sarum Chronicle* 14, 7–36

Universal, 1791–8, *The Universal British Directory of Trade, Commerce and Manufacture*

## Notes

1   WSA Milford T/A
2   Beamon and Roaf 1990, 56
3   Beamon and Roaf 1990, 103
4   WSA CC/Gen/1. This is an archived former catalogue that details records missing from the archive. The records were first transferred in 1963 and 1967 to the Salisbury Diocesan Record Office, then in the Close, and to the Wiltshire Record Office in 1979. At that stage Penelope Rundle, one of the archivists, assigned WRO numbers to the items but she did so by adapting the original catalogue supplied by the Church Commissioners. Therefore the note that certain items are missing dates back to the time of the Church Commissioners' ownership of the collection, rather than having been made since deposit at the WRO. (Claire Skinner, pers. com.)
5   Pigot 1830, 810½ (*sic*)
6   WSA Milford T/A
7   Pigot 1830, 811; Pigot 1842, 32; Slater 1852,
8   Universal 1791–8, 562
9   SJ 16 Sept. 1848, 4
10  David 1996, 310
11  SJ 8 April 1865, 5
12  SJ 7 Sept. 1872, 4
13  Pigot 1842, 30 and 31
14  Ellis 1982, 37
15  Kelly 1880; Kelly 1885
16  Ellis, 1982, 38 and 39
17  Ellis 1982, 44 and 45
18  WSA CC/Gen/1
19  Bailey 1783, 318; Universal 1791–8, 560
20  Pigot 1822, 560, Rogers 1976, 254 and 256
21  Tatton-Brown 2014
22  Chandler 1983, 92

# Images of Longespée a personal view

## David Richards

For nearly 800 years Salisbury Cathedral has displayed the commanding, militaristic tomb of William Longespée (1167 – 1226), 3rd Earl of Salisbury. This paper will look briefly at Longespée's life and attempt to explore how his early images projected his appearance from their creation to the present day. His contemporary images radiated signals of nobility, prestige and soldierly potency. There was no doubt that this was a person of importance who had the means to enforce his will. His heraldic symbols were later to be of interest to antiquarians and historians. In the 19th century Longespée was portrayed as a heroically romantic political figure. A 20th century image shows him as a supporter of the church.

One of the earliest images of Longespée is on his great seal.[1] It shows him galloping vigorously into action, wearing a large flat topped iron helm protected by a massive hinged face piece and wielding his long sword threateningly high around his head. His Plantagenet heritage, his royal blood and lordly status are defined by the panoply of regal lions on his shield and his charger's mantle. Here is a mighty magnate confident in his power to impose his civil and military authority instantly.

The English sculptor Richard Westmacott wrote of the tomb in the 19th century 'the warrior character of this figure is particularly striking'.[2] Even today his sculpture exudes an almost palpable sense of power, of authority, of a mighty warrior confident in his ability and poised to deal with any challenge. In its original glittering condition the gilded chainmail hauberk, the eye-catching azure shield emblazoned with the contemporary (and future) golden beasts of English royalty, the fearsome, eponymous sword and the richly painted plinth all demonstrated his wealth and status as the

Longespée's great seal

son of one of England's most successful kings, Henry II and his mistress Ida. Henry had freely acknowledged William as his natural son, guaranteeing his future position as an influential nobleman and magnate. The tomb effigy of Tournai marble resting on a painted oak chest created after his death in 1226 is in repose. His helmetless head lies half turned on a pillow, his legs at ease, his right arm at his side and his sword sheathed. This apparent inactivity in death belies the undoubted potential power that could formerly have been unleashed against any threat to his position in life. The consummate skills of the unknown sculptor are displayed in the realistic surcoat's folds as they slip, asymmetrically, over a small section of the statue's base. The overall quality of the carving places the tomb amongst the finest surviving church monuments of the early 1200s

And yet his martial appearance illustrates a darker side to the Plantagenet Age. All the kings' great seals depict them mounted on war horses, in armoured battle readiness. In peace time, warlike skills were maintained by the use of the chivalric tournament, with jousting and the mêlée, designed to hone the fighting techniques of the leading elite.[3] In war time the kingdom's security depended on the king's personal strength and military skills and his willingness to maim and kill without compunction. All the barons (including Longespée) were expected to do the same in loyalty to their feudal overlord, the king. Longespée fought, repeatedly and valiantly, placing his life in danger on service for the crown, on campaigns in France, Ireland, Wales and England for over a quarter of a century,[4] achieving victory at Damme[5] before defeat at Bouvines.[6] As Earl of Salisbury he served as Lord High Sheriff of Wiltshire on three separate occasions. King Philip of France's victory at Bouvines saw Longespée bludgeoned from his horse by the Bishop of Beauvais and imprisoned before his return to England. Defeat at Bouvines totally wrecked King John's plans to regain his lost French possessions. Professor Nicholas Vincent writes 'the road from Bouvines to Magna Carta was both straight and speedy'.[7]

When King John's tyranny became unbearable, the barons united and forced the Great Charter on the king at Runnymede. Longespée was named in the Magna Carta as one of John's advisors. But after King John's rejection of Magna Carta, in the Barons' War when he failed to oppose the successful French attack on Winchester, a mere 25 miles from Salisbury, Longespée joined the rebels and Prince Louis. This break came after more than a decade of loyal support to King John and raised the suspicion that Longespée was reacting to the accusation that John (with a justifiable reputation for lechery) had attempted the seduction of Ela Longespée whilst her husband was imprisoned by the French in 1214.[8] However, there was no credible evidence for this and no indication in the royal accounts of costly gifts to Ela or the granting of any favours that might reasonably have been expected from a serial womaniser like King John. It is possible this was malicious gossip spread by the rebels. After John's death he rejoined the crown forces and fought at Lincoln against Prince Louis. Finally it was the hardships Longespée endured leading Henry III's Gascony campaign that

Longespée's tomb (photo Roy Bexon)

An illustration of the tomb of William Longespée in Salisbury Cathedral by Henry Shaw in 1858

eventually contributed to his death in the royal castle of Salisbury in 1226.[9] He was brought in solemn procession from the castle to be the first burial in the newly completed Trinity Chapel in the cathedral. During the 18th century alterations to the church, under Bishop Shute Barrington, the tomb was moved to its present position in the nave. At this time a mummified rat containing traces of arsenic was found within the tomb. This has given rise to the legend that Longespée had been poisoned by Hubert De Burgh when his plan for his nephew to marry Ela Longespée, following Longespée's apparent failure to return from France, had been rejected. But significantly there is no contemporary evidence for this.[10] Indeed, on the contrary, there is evidence that Longespée had grown up and been educated with De Burgh resulting in a friendship and that this good relationship survived the traumas of Magna Carta into the Regency of Henry III. It is reasonable to expect that a suspected murder of such an outstanding war hero and the uncle of the reigning king would have generated accusations, charges and possible arrests. But that did not happen. Perhaps not surprisingly the story of the rat persists to the present as an entertaining myth and shows no sign of abating.

An early heraldic interest in the image was shown by Matthew Paris in 1250 when he included Longespée's coat of arms amongst 42 copies of the shields of members of the English nobility.[11] Much later in 1677, Francis Sandford created a fine Longespée print.[12] Sandford was a herald at the College of Arms and his interest in Salisbury probably was that the stylistic representation of the lions on Longespée's tunic and shield are amongst the earliest public expositions in England of the symbols that were to feature on the royal arms to the present day. A modern reference, illustrated with a photograph, appears in Stephen Slater's *Complete Book of Heraldry* of 2002.[13] In 1755 an Austrian sculptor, Victor Alexander Sederbach produced a series of terracotta statues for the Great Hall of Lacock Abbey. One image, said to be of Longespée, shows him energetically brandishing his great sword.[14] Pevsner describes the statues as 'wild, violent and unrefined'.[15]

During the 19th century there arose a wide spread and passionate interest in the medieval and the Gothic that was reflected in architecture and art throughout England. This in turn sparked renewed fascination with medieval costume and armour. In the 1840s, Henry Shaw, Fellow of the Royal Society of Antiquaries, created a sumptuous painting that showed Longespee's tomb in all the romantic, gilded opulence of its 13th century origin.[16] It was part of the movement that enhanced the growing Victorian perception that the Middle Ages had been a golden age to be admired and respected. Its precision and rich colouring hinted at the direction historical painting was to take in the developing neo-Gothic revival.

Baron William Longespée, fully rounded cast statue by John Evan Thomas © Palace of Westminster Collection WOA S78 www.parliament.uk/art

A contemporary of Shaw's, Samuel Rush Meryrick, a scholar and antiquarian, wrote a lengthy treatise, *A Critical Enquiry into Antient Armour,*[17] in 1842. His romantic colour plate of Longespée shows him in the prime of life looking out of the picture as though listening to an unseen companion. Longespée nonchalantly leans on the hilt of his long sword with his right arm languidly supported by his hip. This was a rare, living, portrayal of a normally fierce and powerful baron looking relaxed and non-threatening. The Victorian explosion of printing saw books, journals, magazines and newspapers generating a strong demand for modern recreations of historic events. Many other engravings depicted Longespée at Runnymede as John signed the Magna Carta. Both actions were unfortunately wrong. Magna Carta was authorized not by a signature but by the king's great seal. There is doubt that Longespée was even present on 15 June 1215.[18] Often in Victorian times whimsical romantic imagination supplanted historical fact.

One of the leaders of the neo-Gothic movement was Augustus Pugin who, whilst living in Salisbury, started his architectural career restoring the Hall of John Hall in the city, and building a house at nearby Alderbury. Pugin's seminal book *Contrasts,* extolling medieval Gothic architecture, was written and published in Salisbury.[19] His fame spread and he joined Charles Barry who was building the new Houses of Parliament. Today, his masterly decoration of the Chamber of the House of Lords contains a statue of William Longespée, 3rd Earl of Salisbury, along with other Magna Carta Barons, gazing down on the political activities of current lords.[20] His depiction as a muscular magnate, bursting with life and the hint of present power, contrasts with his recumbent funereal effigy in Salisbury. His inclusion in the original Magna Carta, his royal lineage, his role as a military commander to King John and King Henry III and his action as one of the founders of Salisbury Cathedral and benefactor to ecclesiastical institutions, justifies his position here, on the right hand of the monarch, next to the golden throne, at every State Opening of Parliament. A plaster maquette of the statue by J Thomas is on display in the Westgate, Canterbury.

An early (if not the earliest) photograph of the tomb is in Gleeson White's *Cathedral Church of Salisbury* of 1898 and is remarkable for the fact that it was taken by a woman, Catherine Weed Ward, an American working in England. She had the rare distinction of being one of the first female professional photographers.

A 20th century post card[21] reconstructs Longespée's victory at the Battle of Damme which inflicted huge losses on the French King Philip II's fleet and resulted in the capture of enormous quantities of supplies and material. As a result Philip was not able to launch his intended invasion of England.

William Longespée, Ela Longespée and Bishop Poore laying foundation stones. Detail from window in Salisbury Cathedral north choir aisle (photo Roy Bexon)

Later during the Barons' War Longespée was closely involved in ejecting Philip's son, Prince Louis, from England.

In the 1980s a Salisbury Cathedral window was designed showing the distinctively armed Longespée, brother of the late King John, on 28th April 1220, laying a cathedral foundation stone on behalf of his nephew, the reigning King Henry III. The Countess Ela, shown alongside him, also laid a stone. Bishop Richard Poore resplendent with mitre and crosier is depicted laying a stone for Pope Honorius III in the Vatican, a stone for Archbishop Langton in Canterbury and a stone for Salisbury. This vignette demonstrates the cooperation of the medieval state and church in a building that would preserve Magna Carta inscribed with Longespée's name, right down to the 21st century. Longespée is seen as supporter and benefactor of the medieval Church of Rome whilst fiercely maintaining his position as an English baron. Unlike all the other images in this paper this one touches on the European significance of England in the 13th century. It is a modern image, in a sketchy, cartoonlike style that connects the present with the very beginnings of New Sarum just after the arrival of Salisbury's own Magna Carta and the subsequent issue of several different versions of the Great Charter.[22]

## Conclusions

Different generations have been drawn to different aspects of his image, ranging from the military, the heraldic, the political and the purely historical. Today in Salisbury, the significance of William Longespée's tomb stems predominantly from its historical associations with Salisbury, Salisbury Cathedral, the Plantagenets and the Earl's role in Magna Carta. But the tomb's intrinsic importance as an historic work of art made it valued by antiquarians, art historians and heraldic scholars. Longespée's stirring life story, his military adventures and his association with King John, King Henry III and Magna Carta have vividly captured the imagination of ordinary people for nearly 800 years. And his evocative tomb continues yet to fascinate. After 800 years, and looking forward to the foreseeable future, Longespée's association with the quintessentially English journey from the medieval rigidity of feudal governance to the liberty and equality of the kingdom's present, uncodified, constitution will assure the immortality of his story.

## Notes

1 www.archive.org accessed March 2015 Bowles, William & Nichols, John, 1835, *Annals & Antiquities of Lacock Abbey*, 147 Longespée's great seal was used on the will he wrote before setting out on the Gascony campaign in 1225.

2 Westmacott, Richard, 1864, *Handbook of Sculpture, Ancient and Modern*, 339 .

3 Pevsner, Nicholas, 1991, The *Buildings of England: Wiltshire* Penguin Books, 488.

4 Strickland, Matthew, 2015, *Dictionary of National Biography* OUP

5 In 1213 Longespée commanded the English fleet attacking King Philip Augustus' anchored ships at Damme (the port for Bruges).

6 In 1214 Philip Augustus defeated John's German and Flemish allies at Bouvines. Longespée, leading the English army, had earlier advised against engaging the enemy. The battle turned out to be a pivotal point in the history of England and France

7 Vincent, Nicholas, 2012, *Magna Carta: A Very Short Introduction*, OUP, 57

8 Strickland, Matthew *ibid* see paragraph headed 'Magna Carta and its aftermath'.

9 Carpenter, DA, 1990, *the Minority of Henry III University* of California Press, 376. Longespée's contribution to military success in Gascony helped to maintain England's presence for there for the next 200 years.

10 Strickland, Matthew *ibid* see paragraph headed 'Last years, death and reputation'.

11 Paris, Matthew, Book *of Additions*, British Library, MS Cott. Nero DI, f.171v

12 Sandford, Francis, 1677, *Genealogical History of the Kings of England*, London. Single engraving held in British Museum.

13 Slater, Stephen, 2002, *The Complete Book of Heraldry* Anness Publishing, 13

14 Ferry, Kathryn, 2013, *A Souvenir Guide, Lacock, Wiltshire* National Trust. It is suggested the image is of William's son, also William. Another Lacock statue, in civilian clothes, holding plans of a church is said to be the 3rd earl. However, positive identification is lacking.

15 Pevsner, Nicholas, 1991, *The Buildings of England: Wiltshire* Penguin Books, 288.

16 www.archive.org accessed January 2015.

17 Meyrick, Samuel Rush, 2007, *Meyrick's Medieval Knights and Armour Dover*

Publications. A reprint of Meyrick's original.

18 Strickland, Matthew *ibid* see paragraph headed 'Magna Carta and its aftermath'.

19 Hill, Rosemary, 2007, *God's Architect,* Allen Lane, Chapter 14 *et al.*

20 www.henry-moore.org/hmi    accessed January 2015 *Database of the Biographical Dictionary of Sculptors in Britain 1660-1851* Notes on John Thomas 1813 – 1862, sculptor of Longespée    and Archbishop Langton in House of Lords. Originally intended to be cast in bronze the cost forced the commissioning of the Birmingham firm of Elkington & Co to cast it in zinc and then electroplate it with copper before gilding. It cost £90.

21 www.mycollectors.co.uk   accessed January 2015. Search for Battle of Damme 1213 Art Postcard.

22 Vincent, Nicholas *ibid* 83-5 An altered Magna Carta 1216 under the seals of Henry III's chief minister, William Marshal and the papal legate Guala 1217. Reissued again under the seals of Marshal and Guala. The involvement of an Italian cardinal emphasized the influence of Europe on the  constitution of England.

# Salisbury's Art Gallery: the first 50 years

## Sue Johnson

Edwin Young (1831-1913) was a local artist who for over 30 years recorded scenes in and around Salisbury with his sympathetic eye and skilled hand. In 1912, towards the end of his life, he indicated his intention to donate his collection of 'about 200 water colour drawings' to the city, together with a suitable building for their exhibition. For the foundation of the gallery and the background of its donor see the author's article 'An Art Gallery for Salisbury' in issue 13 of *Sarum Chronicle*.

Although the choice of a site adjacent to the Library in Chipper Lane and an exterior designed to harmonise with it were sensible enough, the decision that the Gallery would not be an entirely separate building with its own staff, and the failure to set up a separate charity, were to have significant long term consequences. The practical difficulties associated with the Gallery, which consisted of just the two display rooms with no provision for storage, office space, or other facilities, and with the only access through the Library, using its staircase to reach the upper room, soon became apparent. The heating was to be provided as part of the Library's system, but it was found that the existing boiler was not adequate to heat the extra rooms and a new one had to be fitted. The Library Committee's report for 1913–14 said that the cost of the new boiler was 'generously defrayed by Mr. Thomas Young' – he obviously thought otherwise and correspondence on the subject continued for years.[1]

Edwin Young had indicated in 1912[2] his intention to hand over to the City Council the property which was to form the endowment for the Gallery but he neither did so at the time, nor made provision in his will. Following his death (shortly before the Gallery's opening in 1913) it was left to his brother Thomas, his residuary legatee, to make the final arrangements

Fisherton Bridge with the Clock Tower to the right and part of the County Hotel (now the King's Head) to the left. EY61

for its transfer and that of the Gallery two years later.[3] The Clarendon Road houses had been purchased by Edwin and his brother William some years previously but no attempt to put them into a good state of repair before they were used to generate income for the gallery appears to have been made and it was not long before tenants were asking for work to be done, though all internal matters were deemed to be their own responsibility under the terms of their leases.[4]

Repairs were also unexpectedly needed at the Gallery itself, when early in 1916 came the shocking news that the panelling there was rotting due to inadequate ventilation. Inspection by the architect, Mr Blount, revealed the problem to be due to the wood being fixed before the brickwork had thoroughly dried out. He recommended the immediate removal of the infected wood, the city's surveyor concurred, and the room was closed to allow the panelling to be taken away and the walls to dry and be suitably treated.[5] The room remained shut off for the rest of the war. All references so far found appear to suggest it was only the upper gallery which was affected and that the lower room did remain open during this time. In 1919 the City Lands Committee recommended deferring any work on it for the time being due to lack of funds. When the full Council considered the matter Councillor Wort argued that the building was a valuable gift to the city and should be kept in good repair, and it was resolved to get an estimate for the necessary repairs, with the cost to come out of the rates.[6] It was almost another two years before the Librarian could report in October 1921 that 'the repairs to Picture Gallery No. 2' had been finished and three members of the Library Committee were appointed 'to consider the hanging of the pictures.' A year later Miss V Liddell, the Librarian's Assistant, was appointed 'Custodian' of the Picture Gallery with an increase of £20 in her salary, but no details of what her duties entailed were given in the minute recording this event.[7]

In considering the cost of the necessary repairs the point was raised as to whether it was worth spending the money as 'very few people went into the picture gallery'.[8] This issue had surfaced as early as May 1915 when H B Medway suggested that the Gallery be used for lectures as he had always found the room empty of visitors – a view echoed by his colleague Councillor Harrison the following year who stated that he had been several times and never saw another person there – a sharp contrast to the Library Committee's Annual Report in November 1914 when the gallery was said to be 'much frequented by the citizens and visitors'.[9] It is however, entirely logical that there would have been a lot of people visiting at first because it was a new facility, but thereafter, if the display of pictures did not alter, numbers would diminish. There was also the added disadvantage that the galleries, unlike the library, had no electric light. In accordance with Edwin Young's wish to avoid the use of artificial lighting Thomas Young in drawing up the documentation added a clause about the galleries only being open in daylight. The potential difficulties this would cause had been raised when the draft conveyance was discussed in 1913 but in the end the Council had felt obliged to accept it.[10]

One of the many unfinished paintings whose white patches so irritated the Art Gallery committee in 1925. Is the artist perhaps a self portrait? EY350

Although the inscription on the front of the Gallery (presumably chosen by Edwin Young himself) says that it was 'to form the nucleus of an art collection' and the conveyance of the endowment property states that the balance from the income could be used to purchase for it 'paintings by deserving Artists residing in the City of Salisbury or its neighbourhood', this conflicts with the provisions of the conveyance of the Gallery itself which limited its use to housing and exhibiting the collection of pictures painted by Edwin Young and any additions made to it by Thomas Young and forbade the display of any other pictures or its use for any other purpose.[11] When in 1913 the Wiltshire Archaeological & Natural History Society rejected the offer of Edgar Barclay's paintings of Stonehenge due to lack of space they suggested they should go into the new Edwin Young Gallery which was then under construction, but the pictures ended up in the Reading Room. Four of the paintings borrowed from Salisbury Museum in 1919 were supposed to go to the Gallery, but no evidence has been found that they actually did so.[12]

The only known additions to the collection in the early years were those deposited by Thomas Young during his lifetime,[13] which consisted of 'a number of additional pictures', of which no details are given, an antique oak bureau and 'an interesting sword formerly used in the old Salisbury Volunteers', together with those items bequeathed in his will. By this he left 'to the Trustees of my Brother Edwins picture gallery adjoining the Salisbury Public Library' a painting of Salisbury Cathedral from Harnham, the family eight day clock in oak case, by Leach, London, and a walnut cabinet containing a Chubb safe and two violins and bows. These were to remain in the cabinet which was to be glazed to allow them to be viewed easily, with the cabinet being 'kept in the room set apart for my brother's paintings'. The Librarian duly reported to his committee in November that year that the safe with the violins 'is now in place' and a few months later that the clock had been received. In both cases no indication is given of where the items were located in the gallery or library. Neither of these entries mention the painting of Harnham.[14]

Perhaps it was the death of Thomas Young in 1923 which encouraged the Council to disregard the provisos in the conveyance, starting with the installation of electric light in 1924. In September that year a large table for children's use was moved into the lower room, though the Librarian noted that the lack of ventilation there was a problem and that the children 'are apt to play leapfrog over the seats unless closely watched'.[15] That year also saw the formation of a committee to consider alterations in the arrangement of the pictures. This suggested that if fewer were hung at a time the others would show to greater advantage and that 'the unfinished ones, which by their white patches, detract from the rest' should be withdrawn. The proposals were accepted with the suggestion that the rooms should be decorated before the pictures were re-hung. In the meantime a Colour Print Exhibition was to be held in the upper room in February 1925, thus breaching another condition – that only Edwin Young's pictures, or those approved by Thomas Young could be placed in the Gallery. Lack of funds led to delays in redecoration and meant that it was another five months before the upper room was finished, the pictures back on the walls and it was again open to the public. (The lower room had to wait until 1927 before it was painted.) The upper room also gained a table in 1925, principally for the use of the Library Committee whose meetings were in future to be held there.[16]

In 1929 some 150 examples of Contemporary Art were displayed in 'the gallery at the Public Library'. The report of the exhibition in the local paper contained the curious statement that the Chairman of the Library Committee had been surprised when he first came to Salisbury that it

The track at Harnham Bridge. A typical country view which, like many, includes the Cathedral spire. EY322

did not possess a municipal art gallery and implied (notwithstanding the inscription on the outside of the Chipper Lane building) that it still did not. The article also records the thanks expressed to the Library Committee for allowing the exhibition to be held on its premises, but makes no mention of Edwin Young at all, suggesting that his gift had already been forgotten and that the rooms containing the pictures were considered merely as an integral part of the Library.[17]

Since the facilities at the Library were now inadequate due to Salisbury's rising population, 1929 also saw the start of a scheme to improve them. The proposals involved using the lower gallery as a newspaper reading room and the upper one for occasional lectures and exhibitions. Resolving not to act improperly the Council decided to consult the executors of the late Edwin Young's will about their plans, a complicated process which delayed matters for months. The work was finally authorised and by November the Chairman of the Library Committee was able to report that the rearrangement was complete and seemed a great success. The ventilation problem was eventually addressed by making some of the fixed windows into opening ones.[18] The new scheme did not interfere with the display of Edwin Young's pictures, which continued to be hung on the walls of the lower room. The upper room was used for meetings of groups such as the Poetry Circle, occasional evening lectures and for the display of other art works, for example the Salisbury Art Club's exhibition of Contemporary Art in 1930. As well as pictures by nationally known artists such as Augustus John this featured items from local amateurs, including Barbara Townsend's impressionist painting of a corn field, and 'clever lino cuts and pen drawings' by William Hughes, the Librarian and the Club's Honorary Secretary.[19] Greater interest was taken in Edwin Young's paintings with those entering the newspaper reading room and attending lectures frequently inspecting them, whereas previously few visitors ever bothered to look at them.[20]

The new use of the galleries led to criticisms in the local press in 1932 with accusations of neglect of the 'mildewed pictures in their shabby and chipped gilt frames'. In the following week's papers the official viewpoint made it clear that steps were already being taken to remedy the situation when half were found to be 'marked by fungus'. Mr Syms of New Street was the expert engaged to restore the pictures over the next few years. (By 1937 some of them were said to be showing the effects of damp again, suggesting that conditions in the Art Gallery were less than ideal.)[21] There was also a stinging attack on the Council about the new arrangements from one of the donor's nephews, Frank Edwin Young, by now living in Bournemouth. Following various letters to the Council which did not bring about the response he required he then protested in the local press, to the Museums Association and to the Charity Commissioners about the maladministration of the Trust and the flouting of the Founder's wishes by the installation of electric light and taking over the rooms for other purposes.[22] One extremely unwelcome outcome of this campaign was the discovery that although the two conveyances of the Gallery and houses had been sent to the Charity Commissioners for enrolment, because some technical legal point had not been answered, this had not happened at the time. Presumably due to the First World War, with its attendant staff shortages and other pressing matters needing attention, neither Council nor Commission ever followed up the matter, the conveyances never did get enrolled, and therefore they were void. The Commissioners declined to offer an opinion about what effect this had on the Council's authority to decide how the Gallery was used.[23]

Mr F E Young's protests notwithstanding the new use of the rooms continued. The Council not unreasonably pointed out that it was felt unjust that only those at leisure during the day could enjoy the pictures, so electric light had been installed, and that as considerable amounts of public money had had to be spent on the Gallery they should get more use out of it.[24] The original endowment of four houses producing an annual rent of approximately £80 had seemed generous enough in 1913, but it soon became apparent that this was not the case. Thomas Young had arranged, and the Council agreed, that £44 per annum should go to the Public Library Committee to cover supervision (£26), cleaning (£13) and heating (£5). As early as March 1915 it was pointed out that when rates, taxes and insurance on the buildings had been paid this left just over £10 from the current rent of £79–14–0 for repairs and to cover any loss due to the houses being vacant. By May 1916 the administration grant of £44 together with other expenses took up all the income. Proposals to reduce the £44 were unsuccessful so in years when the endowment did not produce insufficient money, it had to come out of Council funds.[25]

The inadequate income from the endowment property left no money to purchase additional pictures for the Gallery but even when paintings were offered to the City Council as a gift the possibility of placing them there never seems to be considered. Thus a watercolour drawing of the Peace Celebration in Salisbury in 1856, given in 1928, went to the Muniment Room. This principle also, rather strangely, applied in 1923 when a new home was being sought for the view of old Fisherton Church by Edwin Young, at that time in the Municipal Offices, which went to Salisbury Museum.[26] A file containing correspondence about Council owned pictures contains numerous rejections of paintings of local interest due to lack of space to hang them, for example the permanent loans, in 1954 and 1959 respectively, of portraits of Bishop Douglas and his wife and a painting of the Guildhall and Guildhall Square. In 1955 the Council pointed out that they already owned 'a number of pictures which they are unable to display and which are stored away in the Guildhall...' A few years later the disposal of

The road to the South Canonry, The Close. EY 164

surplus pictures which could not be shown was under way and it was noted that the Council had not bought any since the last war.[27] Thus although the principle of displaying works by artists other than Edwin Young seems to have been established in the 1920s, the failure to provide suitable storage so that only part of his works were on show, the erosion of the gallery space for Library uses and the lack of funds meant that the opportunity to expand 'the nucleus of an art gallery' given in 1913 was lost.

Salisbury did gain some items of local interest – but for the Library not the Art Gallery. Five 'interesting water-colour drawings by Thomas Wakeman of parts of old Salisbury' were purchased during the 1914–15 financial year, and in 1924 the Library Committee agreed to buy 22 watercolours by E A Phipson, while in the same year Lady Hulse presented 'for use in the Library, a signed copy of the engraving by David Lucas of Constable's very famous picture of Salisbury Cathedral ... known as "Salisbury Cathedral from the Meadows".' Since this was a proof copy, signed by the artist, it was to be screwed to the wall of the reading room.[28] In 1933 Frank Stevens gave the Library an oil painting of a famous local event – the lioness attacking the Mail Coach at the Pheasant Inn, Winterslow, in 1816 – and 20 years later a painting of the Poultry Cross by W Alexander was received.[29]

With the exception of the upstairs gallery being used as a schoolroom during the Second World War there seems to have been little change for many years. The records note routine maintenance work such as redecoration and the 're-surfacing' of the floors so they could be cleaned with an electric polisher,[30] and the use of the lower room for newspaper readers and the upper for occasional meetings and exhibitions continued. The display of Van Gogh reproductions held in conjunction with the WEA in 1948 was poorly attended – perhaps Salisbury was not ready for such modern works, or more likely the lack of publicity was to blame. More successful were the display of photographs of Commerce and Industry by professional photographers in 1950 and of Miss De Vere Temple's pictures of plants, animals and insects two years later, described as 'a delight to the artist and naturalist alike'.[31]

However the overall state of the Art Gallery was evidently not satisfactory. H J Annetts in his Official Visitor's report in March 1949 stated that 'the Young Gallery leaves me with a feeling of abject despair, but I have no concrete suggestions'.[32] Possibly it was this that prompted the re-arrangement of the upper room so that a 'themed' display of 38 views of the Cathedral was on show, instead of the 126 assorted pictures that had previously been there. This display was to be changed every three months, with river scenes, old buildings and villages around Salisbury completing the programme for the coming year.[33] In 1950 six pictures from the Gallery were destroyed due to a leaking roof and two years later the City Engineer reported that the whole asphalt roof needed to be renewed – at a cost several times more than the annual income from the endowment property. General running costs were becoming an increasing burden on local ratepayers. The accounts for 1953–53 make it clear that the amount of £79 paid for supervision, cleaning, lighting and heating (a sum unchanged since 1938–39) was totally inadequate, the actual cost of providing these being at least three times as much.[34]

The Librarian, William Hughes, produced an uncomplimentary note on the current state of affairs in March 1957 saying that Edwin Young's paintings 'presented the appearance of weary wallpaper, a dreary sameness is evident in all the pictures. The passing years have not improved their quality, painted as they were in fugitive colours, and framed in gilt frames long since chipped and tarnished.' He did, however, admit that 'the pictures are not entirely without merit—viewed singly many of them have qualities of charm... [and] As topographical records of places now gone, many of them have value and should be preserved.' In spite of efforts to improve the appearance of the galleries by showing only a selection of works 'Visitors rarely venture beyond the doorway and leave with a very poor opinion of what constitutes

'A Weedy Corner'. Perhaps one of the pictures selected for the 1949 display of Cathedral views. EY338

a Picture Gallery in Salisbury. It is an utter tragedy that Galleries which could be made attractive and give infinite pleasure to many people should, through a dead control, be allowed to fall into disrepair.' The repainting of the lower gallery had transformed the room, but the upper one presented an air of 'gloomy decay'. He suggested removing the pictures from their frames and mounting them in a revolving display or in albums and getting the restrictions on the use of the galleries relaxed to allow exhibitions of art sponsored by the Government or other bodies.[35]

Obviously bearing in mind the protests which had followed the changes to the lower room the Council consulted the Ministry of Education about their proposals. The Ministry's view was that as the 1915 conveyance of the Gallery was void for lack of enrolment, the Corporation had, at the end of 12 years, acquired a possessory title, subject to 'User Trusts' based on the actual uses to which the building had been put, including a) the use of electric light, b) using the lower gallery as a newspaper and magazine room and c) use of both rooms for occasional lectures and exhibitions. The proposal to exhibit pictures other than those in the Young Collection, to show only a selection of the Collection's paintings, the others to be suitably stored, was acceptable and the Corporation were advised to carry out their

Avon Farm, Stratford-sub-Castle. One of the series of pictures which appeared in the 'Then and Now' feature in the *Salisbury Times* to mark the 1961 refurbishment of the upper room. EY 180

proposed changes 'in a reasonable way' and to apply to the Ministry for a formal relaxation of the Trusts if difficulties arose which made this desirable. A subsequent application for permission to use part of the upper gallery as a book store for the Library was rejected, the Ministry feeling that to do so would be in breach of the 'User Trusts' and would render the Corporation liable to legal action.[36]

The upper gallery was redecorated by the City Engineer's department with drab khaki-olive colour walls and green doors giving way to grey walls, blue doors and a pale yellow ceiling with blue panel. New lighting was also installed. The approach eventually adopted for the paintings was to have a small number of frames made, which had removable backs. All the watercolours were to be mounted on standard size boards so that only a few sizes of frame were needed. A selection would be exhibited from time to time and the majority which were not on show, and the frames if they were not in use, were to be stored in a purpose built oak cabinet. Much sorting and measuring of the watercolours went on, including the retrieval of 'about 100 of Mr. Young's paintings at present up in the loft'.[37] The official order for 24 frames went to Noyes & Green of Crane Street, Salisbury, with the mounts provided by Mr Harry Bailey, a retired bookbinder who had previously worked on items for the city archives, and who apparently 'identified the titles'.[38]

A 'rejuvenated' Gallery was officially reopened on 6 June 1961 by the Mayor, Councillor A C Hoy, a member of the Public Library Committee. The invitation to the ceremony stated that 'The Young Gallery ... is now ready to be used for Meetings and Exhibitions, thus becoming a valuable place in the cultural and educational facilities of the City'. Following the success in the upper room a similar approach to the downstairs pictures was suggested.[39] In 1963 matters were finally formalised when the 'Salisbury Picture Gallery' was entered in the Register of Charities.[40]


## Acknowledgements
All images are copyright, and reproduced by kind permission of the Trustees of the Edwin Young Collection.

## Bibliography and Notes
Abbreviations: SJ = *Salisbury & Winchester Journal / Salisbury Journal* ST = *Salisbury Times*
CC&M = Council Chamber & Muniment Room Committee; CLD = City Lands
    Committee; PLB Public Library Committee
At the Wiltshire and Swindon History Centre
G23/100/19, City Council minutes 1911–12
G23/100/20, City Council minutes 1912–13
G23/100/22, City Council minutes 1914–15
G23/100/23, City Council minutes 1915–16
G23/100/26, City Council minutes 1918–19
G23/100/30, City Council minutes 1922–23
G23/100/36, City Council minutes 1928–29
G23/100/40, City Council minutes 1932–33
G23/100/45, City Council minutes 1937–38
G23/100/58, City Council minutes 1951–52
G23/119/10, Library Committee minutes 1915–22
G23/119/11, Library Committee minutes 1922–39
G23/132/16, Clerks Correspondence Files, Young Picture Gallery 1915–69
G23/132/20, Clerks Correspondence Files, Salisbury Library, 1910–1974
G23/132/111, Clerks Correspondence Files, Library 1915–72
G23/132/248, Clerk's Correspondence Files, Guildhall and other Council owned
    pictures 1937–74
G23/152/15, Improvements at Public Library Chipper Lane 1927
G23/890/1, Official Visitors Reports 1906–51
G23/891/1, Librarian's Reports to Committee 1915–27

G23/891/2, Librarian's Reports to Committee 1927–29
G23/891/3, Librarian's Reports to Committee 1929–32
G23/891/4, Librarian's Reports to Committee 1932–35
G23/891/5, Librarian's Reports to Committee 1936–39
G23/891/6, Librarian's Reports to Committee 1939–43
G23/891/7, Librarian's Reports to Committee 1944–47
G23/891/8, Librarian's Reports to Committee 1947–49
G23/891/9, Librarian's Reports to Committee 1949–53
G23/891/10, Librarian's Reports to Committee 1953–62
G23/894/4, Librarian's Correspondence: Edwin Young Collection 1957–74

## Notes

1  ST 1914 Nov 13, p7; various letters in G23/132/20
2  ST 1912 Feb 02, p8
3  G23/100/22, minute 5152, 7 Jan 1915; CC&M minute 121, 19 Feb 1915, records the receipt of the earlier deeds to the houses and picture gallery now F2/2214/40 and G23/150/151
4  SJ 1915, Mch 06, p7; G23/100/22 CLD minute 334, 15 April 1915; G23/100/23, CLD minute 464, 23 June 1916
5  ST 1916 Feb 04, p5; ST 1916 Apl 07, p8
6  ST 1919, Nov 14, p2
7  G23/119/10, 21 Oct 1921; G23/119/11, 20 Oct 1922
8  SJ 1921, Apl 08, p9
9  G23/890/1, 20 May 1915; ST 1916, Jne 08, p8; ST 1914, Nov 13, p7
10  ST 1913, Aug 08, p8
11  Copy of conveyances in G23/132/16
12  WAM 38 (1913-14), p121; G23/100/20, CC&M minute 51, 19 Sept 1913; G23/100/26, CC&M minute 294, 16 May 1919
13  G23/100/22, CC&M minute 132, 23 April 1915
14  Will of Thomas Young, of Milford Hill Cottage, Salisbury, who died 6 Jan 1923, proved 6 July 1923; G23/100/30, CLD minutes 1849 & 1884, 20 July 20 & 26 Oct 1923; G23/891/1, 16 Nov 1923 & 20 June 1924
15  G23/891/1, 19 Sep 1924
16  G23/891/1, Sep 1924; Mch & Jly 1925; G23/119/11, Jne, Jly, Sep, Nov & Dec 1924, Mch, Apl, Jne, Jly & Sep 1925; G23/152/15. The contract for painting etc specifies that the woodwork is to be 'the present colour' (not given) and the walls green
17  ST 1929, Mch 08, p7; ST 1929, Mch 22, p8
18  Various items in G23/132/16; ST 1929 Nov 15, p8; G23/890/1, 27 Jan 1930
19  ST 1929, Nov 15, p8; G23/891/3, Mch, Oct & Dec 1930; ST 1930 Mch 21, p8
20  ST 1932 Jly 22, p2
21  ST 1932 Jly 15, p2 & 22, p2; G23/891/3, May & Jne 1932; G23/891/4, Oct 1932 & Feb 1934; G23/891/5, Sep 1937
22  Assorted letters in G23/132/16; SJ 1933 May 12, p9
23  Letter dated 30 Apl 1930 in G23/132/116. No steps to clarify the legal position with regard to the Gallery appear to have been taken following the receipt of this

information
24 Letter to Ministry of Education 9 Apl 1957 in G23/894/4
25 SJ 1915, Mch 06, p7; G23/100/23, CLD minute 453, 19 May 1916
26 G23/100/36, minute 11367, 9 Nov 1928; G23/100/30, minute 8770, 7 Jne 1923
27 G22/132/248, 7 Sep 1954, 1 Jne 1955, 30 Jly 1959, 29 Sep 1966
28 Annual Report of the Library Committee, loose copy in G23/100/22; G23/119/11, 20 Jne 1924; ST 1924 Nov 28, p2; G23/891/1, 20 Jne 1924. The present Edwin Young Collection contains 10 Phipson watercolours, perhaps the remnants of this acquisition.
29 ST 1933 Oct 06, p5; G23/891/10,13 Nov 1953
30 G23/891/6, 17 Nov 1939; G23/100/40, PLB minute 681, 11 Nov 1932; G23/100/45, PLB minute 1123, 8 April 1938, minutes 1131 & 1132, 13 May 1938
31 G23/891/8, Sept & Nov 1948; ST 1950 Sep 22, p8 & 10; ST 1952 Oct 22, p1
32 G23/890/1, 11 Mch 1949
33 G23/891/8, 11 Mch & 6 May 1949; SJ 1949 Apl 08, p6
34 G23/891/9, Nov 1950; G23/100/58, PLB minute 2051, 11 Jan 1952; G23/132/16, accounts included in letter to Ministry of Education 9 April 1957
35  G23/894/4, assorted papers
36 G23/894/4, copy of letter to Ministry of Education dated 9 April 1957; notes on meetings there 10 Dec 1957 and 31 Dec 1959
37 Memo fr City Librarian to City Engineer, 9 Sep1960, in G23/894/4
38 SJ 1961 Jne 09, p17; assorted items in G23/894/4, mostly not dated but all about 1960; frame order dated 1960 Dec 08; estimate for mounting approximately 300 watercolours from H Bailey, Queensberry Rd, dated 1959 Oct 24 [sic, though probably incorrect, the letter asking him for an estimate is dated 14 Oct 1960]
39 G23/894/4 invitation letter dated 1961 May 29; 1961 SJ Jne 09, p17; ST Jne 09, p5; G23/891/10, Dec 1961
40 G23/894/4 Letter from Ministry of Education to Town Clerk, 19 June 1963

Buildings dating from the 17th century form today's Abbaye aux Dames in Saintes, which was founded as a convent in 1047 and now houses an important music con-servatorium

# Twenty-five years of entente cordiale

## Caroline Rippier

Travel broadens the mind, and there is no denying that travel can be enriched by the people you meet. If you enjoy their company, it is easy to see how that experience can be further enhanced if you are guaranteed a welcome and you make new friends each time you go to the same place. That is one of the ways in which town twinning works.

Salisbury came late to the idea of twinning. It is a concept that was established after the Second World War to help promote understanding and friendship between people from different countries. Despite watching other places in the area tie the knot with towns in France in the 60s and 70s, Salisbury remained resolutely unattached.

For example, Devizes has been twinned with Mayenne since 1963, Warminster with Flers (1973), Shaftesbury with Brionne (1974) and Fordingbridge with Vimoutiers, the home of Camembert, since 1977. Some of these towns also have formal arrangements with towns in Germany and elsewhere.

While Salisbury itself was twinless, however, the city's Rotary Club established links with the Rotary Club of St Germain-en-Laye in north-central France in the 1950s, and the Diocese of Salisbury with the Diocese of Evreux in Normandy in the 1980s.

It was not until 1989 that Salisbury's incoming mayor, Cllr Margot Jackson, discovered a letter in a District Council desk drawer from someone in Saintes (pronounced Sant), in the Charente-Maritime in south-west France. Margot's attention was caught by its subject, which concerned the possibility of an official twinning. She persuaded her fellow councillors that it would be a good thing and on St George's Day, 23 April 1990, the official document was signed in the Guildhall, Salisbury. A civic delegation from Saintes witnessed the ceremony and the framed document can still be seen in the Guildhall.

Three months later, a similar document was signed in Saintes. In addition to the name of the Mayor of Saintes, it also bears the signature of Salisbury's mayor who had taken up office after Cllr Jackson, Cllr Kay Cooper Joel. It is worth noting that Saintes already had quite an impressive list of twins: there was already Xanten in Germany, making for a three-way or ring link with Salisbury, as well as Cuevas in southern Spain, Vladimir in Russia, Nivelles, Belgium, and Tombouctou, Mali.

It was in 2006 that Salisbury and Xanten became officially twinned. Both Saintes and Xanten are famed for their history and their Roman remains and, like Salisbury, attract tens of thousands of tourists annually. Salisbury's Cathedral, the Close, the half-timbered medieval buildings and pubs and our proximity to Stonehenge and the New Forest combine to ensure that our

The iconic Roman amphitheatre in Saintes was designed to seat 15,000 spectators, the town's population at the time. It dates from *c*40 AD

The Mayor of Salisbury, Cllr Andrew Roberts, in his role as president of the Salisbury Saintes Twinning Association, hands over an anniversary greeting to Ian Standen to be taken to the Mayor of Saintes. Ian is chairman of Salisbury Motorcycle and Light Car Club, more than a dozen of whose members went to Saintes this summer and were hosted by members of the club there

twinning friends enjoy their trips here, to say nothing of the warm welcome they always receive.

Every formal twinning requires an active twinning association to make things work. Run by volunteers, such an association will succeed or fail because of the people involved. In fact Cllr Jackson admitted thinking, as she signed the first document, that it might last two or three years, at most. Nevertheless, Salisbury Saintes Twinning Association (SSTA) thrives these days and has a membership of slightly less than 100. With the aim of 'fostering cultural, educational, sporting and commercial links', there is plenty of scope to interest people from all walks of life.

A cynic might say that twinning is only about councillors going on jollies at public expense. Others would counter that accusation by listing the many combined initiatives that have taken place and that have been of benefit to both communities.

Just imagine how the economy was boosted when a group of 40 ramblers from the Saintes area came to Salisbury and stayed at the much missed former Youth Hostel. They ate at the YHA, as well as in local hostelries, and bought presents to take home. On the other side of the English Channel,

The two buildings that form the 19th century Hôtel de Ville in Saintes are linked by a striking contemporary glass extension

one can see how 80 members of Salisbury Area Young Musicians will have given a boost to the places they visited in July 2014. They performed in Saintes and nearby towns.

Apart from boosting both economies, it is thanks to twinning links and contacts that a Salisbury student has been able to spend six months teaching at a lycée in Saintes, and a business student from Saintes has spent valuable time volunteering in several departments at a Salisbury charity.

Another undergraduate who was at school in Salisbury spent a summer in Saintes during a university vacation, working at the Saintes Music Festival and then in the town's busy tourist office.

Over the years there have been school visits on both sides of the Channel, and Salisbury even welcomed Miss Saintes one summer while she improved her English. She arranged her own internship with Salisbury Chamber of Commerce but also visited schools, answered questions from pupils, and presented prizes at the primary schools' athletics competition, clad in her favourite dress which she had bought in Salisbury. She proudly wore her tiara and sash of office even when she climbed the Cathedral tower.

Not all our visitors are so distinguished, but among many we have welcomed have been a choral group which attracted appreciative crowds to the bandstand during the first chilly weekend of one of the city's Christmas markets. On that occasion, the Mayor of Salisbury hosted them afterwards at a welcoming soup-and-sandwich lunch in the Grand Jury Room upstairs at the Guildhall.

Salisbury Cathedral choir has visited Saintes twice (in 2009 and 2014), and in 2013 the organist of Cathédral St Pierre in Saintes gave a recital in Salisbury.

In common with the Salisbury Xanten Twinning Association, the SSTA always welcomes the current city mayor as its president during their year of office. Some years are busier than others, with Guildhall receptions for visiting groups as varied as ramblers and horticulture students. All are impressed by the Guildhall and by the Mayor's beautiful chain.

European mayors tend not to go in for much in the way of regalia. Tricorn hats, brightly coloured robes and mayoral chains are a novelty to them, for the only thing that most of them have to show for their position is a sash in their national colours, worn either across the body or in the style of a wide belt.

Mussels (and muscles?) for sale in the twice-weekly market held in the shadow of the Cathédrale St Pierre

Music while you spend: a tuneful accompaniment provided by three cheerful musicians in the market

In 2013, with the 25th anniversary of the Saintes twinning looming, Salisbury City Council voted to give both twinning associations £1500, spread over three years, to assist with hospitality and other expenses. The SSTA has, in recent years, introduced awards to offer to students at member schools. Such an initiative has proved popular and successful. It encourages the learning of French and helps promote twinning. In addition, a special bursary to mark the 25th anniversary has been offered to a Year 12 French-language student to help them improve their French in Saintes in the summer holiday.

It is cause for regret that no South Wiltshire businesses have so far availed themselves of commercial opportunities in Saintes, a place with a rich cultural heritage that is also home to many anglophiles and many ex-pat British people. There is great enthusiasm for all things English and particularly for anything connected with Salisbury.

There have been numerous sporting exchanges, whether it was this year's cyclists visiting Salisbury, and a group of Salisbury motorcyclists going to

What would a French market be without 'escargots'?

Saintes, or young Salisbury rugby enthusiasts playing matches over a long weekend in past years. Tennis, Morris dancing, choirs, folk dancing, lace-making, light opera, fine art, cinema have all played their part in building friendships.

The magnificent Arc de Germanicus (18 -19 AD) was moved stone by stone in 1843 from its position on the old bridge across the Charente river, before being rebuilt in its current position on the river bank

Artists from Saintes have taken part in Salisbury Art Trail, and there have been exhibitions of Salisbury artists' work in Saintes. A year-long artefact swap between Saintes archaeological museum and The Salisbury Museum also took place.

Saintes may not be the easiest of places to reach by road. It is, after all, 375 miles south of Salisbury, but it is in a fascinating area near the coast with its oyster beds and beautiful beaches, vineyards, great food, and many other attractions. It is not too far from Cognac, Bordeaux, and Poitiers, birthplace of King John's mother, Eleanor of Aquitaine, and Angoulême, where Isabella, his second wife, was born.

The SSTA meets informally each month in a city-centre hotel for chat and an exchange of information. Talks and visits to places of interest locally that might have a French connection, however tenuous, are arranged and there is always the annual dinner to look forward to, wine-tastings, a barbecue held in a member's garden (the sun always shines), and travel opportunities.

General-interest trips for groups of 60 people packed into a coach tend not to appeal these days. The last of those was in 1998. Nowadays members often go by car via Portsmouth and Channel ferry, but the flight from Southampton to La Rochelle is another option with a 40-minute car journey to Saintes from the airport. Whichever method of travel is used, in the past 25 years there have been countless visits and exchanges during which new friendships have been made, and old friendships renewed.

www.salisburysaintestwinning.co.uk

All photographs are © the author.

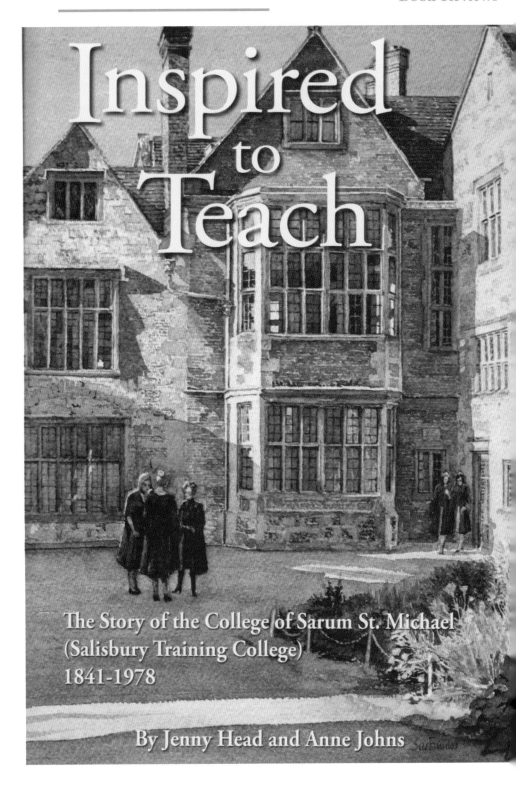

# Inspired to Teach

The Story of the College of Sarum St. Michael
(Salisbury Training College)
1841-1978

By Jenny Head and Anne Johns

# Inspired to Teach
# The Story of the College of Sarum St Michael (Salisbury Training College) 1841-1978

## by Jenny Head and Anne Johns

Ex Libris Press 2015  ISBN 978–1–906641–79–5  304pp  £25.00

This account of the educational training college in Salisbury's Cathedral Close is a labour of love written by two past students, Jenny Head and Anne Johns, who have produced a well-detailed and richly illustrated history. They not only do justice to their subject but also provide interesting cross-references to local, national and international developments including those that contributed to the College's foundation, to its development and, sadly, to its closure.

The Bishop of Salisbury, The Rt Rev'd Nicholas Holtam, provides the foreword. In so doing he maintains the tradition of the caring support the Church of England has consistently provided for state education in England since the early nineteenth century. In 1840 the Salisbury Diocesan Board of Education responded promptly to the request made by the National Society to establish provision for teacher training and so ensure the availability of trained staff for the growing number of schools. After dialogue with the Winchester Diocese (which proceeded to establish a training college for men) Salisbury decided a 'Training School for Mistresses' would be founded. This became a reality in 1841 as the first institution in the country to be founded specifically for women, with the principle of instruction in a Christian calling.

From its early days in different houses in The Close, its move to the King's House in 1855 and its development there and in other buildings, the College benefited from dedicated staff and committed students. This history records the decades when conditions for the students were severe, with inflexible rules, poor diets, Spartan living quarters and compulsory housework of industrial proportions. Thomas's Hardy's sisters Mary and Kate underwent these experiences, but with time and more enlightened attitudes matters improved.

After daily attendance at Cathedral services, the building of the College Chapel of the Holy Angels in 1898 gave the staff and students their own place of worship. It was a significant example of the ways the College grew in response to the demands of the state, such as the 1870 Education Act. With growing links to St. Martin's and St. Edmund's Schools, the College became a very important Salisbury institution, The authors quote Bishop John Wordsworth in 1901 giving his view that the College 'must rank as one of the very highest influences of her late Majesty's reign'.

Coping with the effects of two world wars, economic depression, periods of harsh weather and the changing demands of the state, thoroughly trained and motivated teachers continued to benefit from their time at Salisbury Diocesan Training College – or the College of Sarum St. Michael as it became in 1965 – until its apparently unavoidable closure in 1978.

Jenny Head and Anne Johns have included a wealth of documents, photographs and personal testaments that are witnesses to the valued importance of the College to its alumnae and their teachers. The continuing camaraderie in the celebratory reunions of past students is also evident in this book. Sponsorship of the publication by the Chalke Valley History Trust is a fitting recognition of the work of the authors and the worth of their subject.

John Cox

# Barley to Bayonets: A Biography of Nineteenth-Century Bulford, Before the Soldiers Arrived

## by Peter Ball

Hobnob Press, 2015. 365pp, paperback, £12.95, ISBN 978–1–906978–21–1

Peter Ball spent time in Bulford as a child before returning as a teacher in the village school in the 1970s. Although soon to move away again, his interest in the village and the area was deeply felt and led to years of research into its history, culminating in this book. Sadly, Peter died shortly before it could be published, and a touching tribute from friends precedes the text.

*Barley to Bayonets* tells the story of a small rural village through the nineteenth century, not just by considering the most significant places and people, but by carefully assimilating a vast array of records involving or affecting the lives of everyone who lived there into an unusually engaging and thoroughly researched book.

Links with neighbouring parishes and even Canada have been painstakingly investigated, and many detailed family histories, to the level where Ball knew the location and profession of everyone born in Bulford in the period, even when they had left the parish. The sources range from the expected, such as the census and church records, to personal notebooks and accounts, records of the estate and workhouse, all framed in a wider and sometimes national context. They are used to tell a clearly evidenced story rather than being presented for their own sake, while extensive endnotes provide full references.

The book is broken into chapters looking at different features of village life and how they changed during the period, concluding with a glimpse of the radical changes that occurred following the permanent arrival of the army.

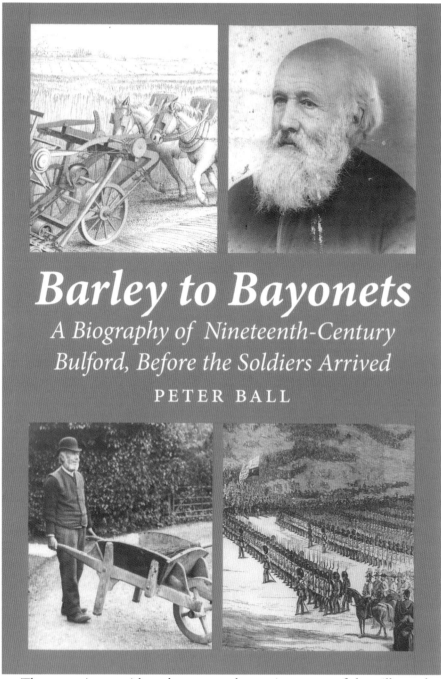

**Barley to Bayonets**
A Biography of Nineteenth-Century
Bulford, Before the Soldiers Arrived
PETER BALL

The scene is set with a chapter on the environment of the village, also helpfully describing how it has changed since the period of the book, its residents and their jobs. We learn of the quality of their lives, which most certainly was not easy. The dampness of the village at the confluence of two rivers was credited with widespread rheumatism, while firewood to combat damp in the cottages was very expensive due to the lack of woodland on Salisbury Plain. Poverty was rife in agricultural villages in the early C19 and Bulford did not escape its challenges: we hear stories of poaching and the stealing of potatoes, and the hardships faced, but also from the contrasting inventories and recipes of the lady of the Manor. William Cobbett visited in 1826 and quotes are drawn from his observations of the village, describing 'general extreme poverty'; a report on buildings in 1860s makes it clear that little had changed. We learn about the impact of mechanisation of agriculture, from the period of the Swing Riots that directly affected farmers in Amesbury and Durrington but not Bulford, to the loss of income from handspinning, and subsequent changes in the way sheep were used on the downs, drawn from newspaper articles and detailed analysis of extensive local farm records.

Church and chapel stories are told from a variety of first hand accounts, describing how Bulford's parishioners were poorly served by the church, the subsequent establishment of the chapel and its links with a Canadian preaching family. This section is peppered, as throughout the book, with interesting and often entertaining anecdotes such as the churchwardens' objections to Lady Pollen grazing her horses in the churchyard, and the rebuilding of the chapel only twenty years after its construction due to imminent collapse. Ownership and inheritance of the village lands by the Seymour family of East Knoyle and the Southbys, as lords of the manor, is detailed. Anthony Southby was variously a doctor in England and Canada, a zoologist and biologist of national repute, and later applied his scientific skills to papermaking at Bulford's watermill, the story of which began in the mid eighteenth century using rags from Salisbury.

The arrival of the army, and with it the railway, changed the focus of village life entirely, with decreasingly viable agricultural landholdings forcing farmers out of business, villagers travelling further afield to work in service, and the camp's huge demand for labour and servicing providing new employment.

Appendices provide several full family trees, lists of church and chapel officials, further information on papermakers and two pieces of writing by Prudence Sawyer, a member of one of the prominent families who was born in 1879.

*Barley to Bayonets* is a fascinating and meticulously researched book which successfully invites the reader to imagine what it would have been like to live in or visit Bulford during the nineteenth century, and to understand so much more about the village today. A real pleasure to read, it will clearly be of interest to those who know Bulford and its neighbours, but there will also be resonances with many other villages of the Plain, and I would highly commend it to anyone looking for an exemplary work of local history.

Andrew Minting

# Salisbury Silver

## Richard Deane

While Salisbury is fortunate in its wealth of surviving historic buildings, the fact that these are mostly houses obscures its former importance as a place to work in, and the diversity of the resulting occupations. The Salisbury silversmiths have been erased from the city's memory as thoroughly as any other of its lost trades. A case in Salisbury Museum has three spoons and two bowls the only public clue locally to an activity for which Salisbury was, for a time, one of the most important centres in the country.[1] This piece will try to set out how silver making in Salisbury fitted into the national context, how some of its practitioners came to local prominence, and the forms of its most important products. It will also illustrate an element of lawlessness and sharp practice that incurred the displeasure of the London-based guardians of the trade, in a recurring cycle of transgression, rebuke and false contrition that sometimes came close to farce.

The story only really starts after the Reformation. There were clearly silversmiths at work in the city in the middle ages, since an Act of 1423 which allowed for the establishment of assay offices in seven provincial places included Salisbury among them, but no pieces known to have been made there before the Reformation have survived. It is not clear whether the assay office was ever set up (there certainly wasn't one after the Reformation), and there is very little information about the silversmiths of the medieval period. The churchwardens' accounts of St Edmund's and St Thomas's mention James Goldsmythe and Robert Goldsmyth, but only in the context of repairing existing items.[2]

This lack of information is a shame, because within our area there is a unique concentration of silver of pre-Reformation period. The major work by Charles Oman, *English Church Plate*, lists no more than 30 pre-Reformation chalices made in this country and still owned by parish churches, with a further 30 or so in other hands.[3] Of the parish church ones there are two

Chalice from St Mary's, Wylye, made in London in 1525. Height 6.75", with original gilding. Photograph by Peter Marsh

in Dorset, and none at all in Hampshire or Berkshire.[4] The main anomaly is Wiltshire, with six surviving chalices. Four of these are from villages west of Salisbury, namely Wylye, Codford St Mary, Ebbesbourne Wake and Berwick St James.[5] The significance of this survival will be considered later.

While the Reformation ultimately had major consequences for parish church silver, in Salisbury as elsewhere, the disappearance of medieval vessels was not due to Henry VIII. His seizures of ecclesiastical property were never extended to parish churches.[6] This was left to Edward VI, as evidenced by a record which states that on March 3rd 1551 'It was decreed that forasmuch as the Kinges Majestie had need presently of a masse of money, therfore commissioners shulde be addressed into all the shires of England to take into the Kinges handes such church plate as remaigneth, to be emploied unto his Highnes use'.[7]

The principle actually adopted was that all churches should be left at any rate one chalice, and that if they had two or more the one they kept would be the 'least' or 'worst'. Wealthy city churches such as St Thomas's and St Edmund's would have suffered serious losses, but the average country church generally had just one chalice, and so was little affected.[8]

Once the brief counter-Reformation under Mary was over, and Protestantism restored under Elizabeth I, a very large number of medieval chalices would still have survived.[9] Their rarity now has nothing to do with monarchs seeking 'a masse of money', and everything to do with concern among the church authorities at the readiness of people to return to the old ways under Mary. One response was a requirement for 'massing chalices' to be replaced by 'decent communion cups'.[10] The former were pre-Reformation vessels which would have been seen as papist survivals and reminders of former times, such as the superb example from Wylye, and the latter were much less showy Elizabethan cups, such as the typical one, probably made in 1598, belonging to Trinity Hospital in Salisbury.[11] This organised process of replacement saw the vast majority of medieval chalices melted down.

The campaign proceeded on a diocese by diocese basis rather than all at once, presumably to avoid overloading the London silversmiths who made most of the new cups. Dorset, which was then in Bristol diocese, saw them come in mostly during the years 1570–1574, with Salisbury diocese following in 1576 and 1577. Both Dorset and Wiltshire have a significant number of cups which were not made in London, lacking the full set of hallmarks associated with the capital. Some Dorset ones have a mark showing they were made by a Dorchester silversmith, but large groups in both counties bear either no mark, or a 'maker's mark' not definitively linked to any known person.[12] That these cups were made in Salisbury is a relatively recent discovery.[13]

A cup from Gillingham in Dorset belongs to the Salisbury-made group, and comparing it with the Trinity Hospital one shows the key Salisbury characteristics. The first point of difference is the knop, the projection on the stem, which in most Elizabethan cups is symmetrical and midway between base and bowl. In the Salisbury type the knop is asymmetrical and

Communion cup from Trinity Hospital, Salisbury, probably made in 1598. Height 6.5".
A typical cup of the standard Elizabethan type. Photograph by Peter Marsh

immediately below the bowl, and has a rope or cable moulding under it.
The second Salisbury feature concerns the decoration on the bowl, of a type
known as strapwork. On Salisbury cups this is of a more elaborate pattern

Communion cup from St Mary's, Gillingham. Date of 1574 on cover. Height 8". A typical Salisbury-made cup in style, though exceptionally large. Photograph by Peter Marsh

than usual, but without the added flourishes, known as foliation, found on typical Elizabethan ones.

The Gillingham cup is one of those with a maker's mark on it. This is the 'pelleted circle', which is central to our story, even if much about it remains unexplained. 'Pellet' in this case refers to raised dots. Of 20 Elizabethan cups in Dorset known to have been made in Salisbury, 13 carry this mark. In Wiltshire there are 16 cups of this type, but only one of them, from

The pelleted circle mark, on a cup from Chalbury in Dorset. Diameter 0.25". Photograph by Richard Deane

Corsley near Warminster, has the mark.[14] It is a remarkably frustrating piece of evidence, with no logic in having the mark on some pieces but not on others clearly from the same workshop, and with no real indication as to whom it belonged. The Gillingham cup has a date 1574, and the mark also appears on spoons whose style points to their being made 50 or 60 years later, or more, suggesting that it was passed on from one maker to at least one other.

There is one obvious candidate for the first of these makers, but again the picture is confused. An entry in the 1569 minutes of the Goldsmiths' Company says 'Received of Thomas Atkyns of Salisburie, goldsmythe, for a fyne of a Communion Cuppe worse 7 dwts....'.[15] The last part indicates use of sub-standard silver, a subject returned to later. Thomas Atkins was a prominent citizen, mayor of Salisbury in 1570/1 and known from tax records and his will to have been well off.[16] He is an obvious candidate for chief communion cup maker of his time in Salisbury, but as he died in October 1576 he could not have been responsible for all the cups in the peak years for Wiltshire of 1576 and 1577, let alone some which are known to be later. Further confusion comes from a Salisbury cup from Manningford Bruce in the Vale of Pewsey, which uniquely has a mark 'TA' or 'AT'. If this refers to Thomas Atkins (and there is no other known candidate), why he should have put it only on one item is inexplicable.

The area in which Salisbury cups of the Elizabethan period are found comprises east Dorset and south Wiltshire, with some extension northwards.

There is a probable outlier in the far west of Dorset, with two cups in Hampshire, one in south Somerset, and three in Berkshire (which was in Salisbury diocese till 1836).[17] The total number of known Salisbury-made cups surviving from this period is 41, plus one or two uncertain cases.

Given all the pressure for change, it is reasonable to wonder why four pre-Reformation chalices survived west of Salisbury. Some connection is likely with the long-standing Roman Catholic influence in the Tisbury area, focused on Wardour Castle and the Arundell family which owned it, and visible now at the splendid Catholic chapel at Wardour, and the Catholic cemetery half a mile away.[18] How much further the story can be taken

Chalice from St Mary's, Sturminster Marshall, made in London in 1536, and altered in Salisbury c1570-4. Height 6.75". Photograph by Peter Marsh

is unclear. Documentary evidence explaining how the chalices survived is unlikely, and it's a matter of guesswork whether they remained in full view throughout, or whether that they were hidden away until pressures for change had subsided.

The pattern of survival provides no real clue, with no medieval silver at any of the churches in the immediate Wardour area. Perhaps the proximity to each other of Wylye, Codford and Berwick St James, slightly further from Wardour, is a clue to some completely unrecorded factor, or perhaps there was just a particular strain of cussedness in that part of the Wylye valley, and a determination to hang on to familiar silver vessels. Religious sentiment, of any doctrinal form, may not necessarily have been key to these beautiful things surviving.

There is one other cup which, while not exactly a Salisbury product, has a connection with the city, and tells a very unusual story.[19] One of the two pre-Reformation chalices surviving in Dorset is from Sturminster Marshall, west of Wimborne. This chalice was made in London in 1536, but there is more to it than that. While most parishes were dutifully replacing such chalices, and a very small number stubbornly held on to them, Sturminster Marshall church adopted a unique middle course, by having the most lavishly decorative part of theirs, which was the knop between the bowl and the base, replaced with a much more restrained one. Above the base, an area of fused and blurred silver is the remains of decoration similar to that above the base of the Wylye chalice. And below the newly added knop is a rope or cable moulding, exactly as on the Salisbury-made communion cups, plus one above.

The inescapable conclusion is that the Sturminster Marshall chalice was taken to Salisbury to be altered, after which it was near enough to the 'decent communion cup' type to escape censure. This remarkable hybrid, London work of 1536 above and below and Salisbury work of probably about 40 years later in the middle, is an encapsulation of a whole episode in religious and social history, momentous in its immediate impact, and long-lasting in its effects.

Communion cups continued to be made in Salisbury in the 17th century, with some half a dozen examples known. One of these, from Sopley in Hampshire, is particularly significant, because it has the rope moulding, and also the mark of a leading Salisbury silversmith called Robert Tyte, proving that the moulding was a Salisbury motif.[20] However by now the chief focus of the Salisbury makers was spoons, as was often the case outside London. A significant number of them survive, to illustrate the story of Salisbury silver in the 17th century.

Details of the careers of over a dozen Salisbury silversmiths have now been established.[21] The best-known of all of them is John Ivie, one of the most notable citizens in the city's history, who as mayor during the plague year of 1627 stayed and did what he could to combat the disease, while most who were in a position to do so fled.[22] A spoon made by him can be seen in Salisbury Museum, but little is known about his silversmithing activities, and they may not have been his chief source of income.

Between Atkins in 1570/1, and Ivie, who did the job again in 1647/8, a third Salisbury silversmith, George Churchouse, became mayor in 1617/8. Besides Robert Tyte, who as well as the Sopley communion cup made a large number of spoons, other notable figures in the trade in the years up to the Civil War included Thomas Hooper and John Greene. Hooper died fairly young, in 1640, and a year later his widow married Greene. The latter's first wife had been a daughter of George Churchouse, and there are other instances of family connections between members of the trade. Tyte, for instance, was John Ivie's uncle. No women are recorded among the practising silversmiths.

The figure below shows a group of typical Salisbury spoons from this period. Two of them are of the type known as seal tops, from the decorative finials which terminate in something resembling a seal, though they were not used for this. The left-hand spoon has a fairly elaborate finial, while the central one has a simpler one. Spoons with finials of both types are found

Group of three Salisbury-made spoons, period 1620-1650. Length of central spoon 7". Photograph by Peter Marsh

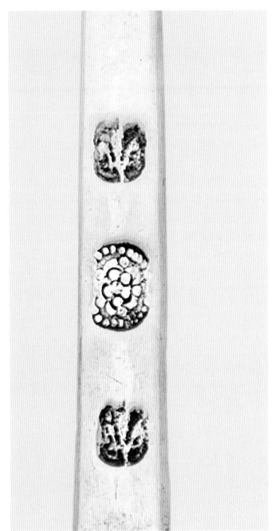

Marks on rear of L/H spoon in previous illustration. Compare pelleted circle mark here with that on the cup from Chalbury illustrated earlier. Photograph by Peter Marsh

in considerable numbers, and are typically around 7" long. While the main bodies were made from a single piece of silver, the finials were cast separately, and then soldered on. The other spoon is a much rarer type known as a slip top. 'Slip' is an old word meaning 'prune', so its use here is from the way the top of the stem is cut off, at an angle.

All three of these spoons carry the pelleted circle mark, though in the case of the two seal tops this is a more complex variant of the one enlarged earlier. The significance of this variation is no clearer than other aspects of the mark. As well as its standard position on the bowl, on the left-hand spoon it also appears on the underside of the stem, together with two fleur-de-lys marks, occasionally found on other silver with a Salisbury connection. The central spoon has two 'pricked' inscriptions, formed by a series of dots. The one on the top of the seal shows double 'I' initials, which may stand for 'J's. These are repeated under the bowl, together with a date, perhaps 1657 but unfortunately rather blurred. Spoons with a single set of initials are likely to have been baptismal presents, while the ones often found with two sets would have been wedding presents.

The central and right-hand spoons have bowls whose elegant shape is very typical of this period, whereas the more symmetrical bowl of the left-hand spoon is less common. The number of surviving Salisbury spoons is such that in the view of the leading authority on Salisbury silver, Tim Kent, 'During the 25 years before the Civil War Salisbury was indubitably the largest centre of spoonmaking outside London'.[23] Exeter would have been next in line, with no other town coming near. Salisbury's status in this field must be a reflection of its continuing importance among English cities. John Chandler has shown it as probably the seventh largest in the country from the 14th century through to the early part of the 16th.[24] By 1661 it had declined to the fifteenth largest, but the real downhill slope only came after that. The opportunities it provided for silversmiths, lifting it in that field higher than its overall economic status, may have been due to the persistence of a reputation for silver making from the middle ages. The Act of 1423, with its reference to the city as a place which merited having an assay office, shows that silver was being produced there, and perhaps Salisbury's prominence then was equal to its status later on. So little medieval silver has survived that there is no way of knowing for sure.

For the later period Tim Kent has unearthed a remarkable story from the archives of the Goldsmiths' Company, starting from long-term suspicion as to what provincial silversmiths were up to. Where there was no local assay office, as at Salisbury in the post-Reformation period at least, and where it was impractical for silver to be sent to London to be certified, these makers were obliged by the oath of 'Strangers Goldsmiths of the Country' to observe various requirements.[25] The most critical was to use only silver of sterling standard, which was based on the Troy ounce, subdivided into 20 pennyweight. The standard was 11 ounces two pennyweight of silver to 18 pennyweight of other metal, in practice copper, which was needed to give the alloy greater rigidity. This translates to metal with a minimum silver content of 92.5%.

The Company's strategy to try to control provincial silversmiths was to carry out 'searches', which were spot checks by wardens from London.[26] Testing would be done 'by the touch', whereby quality was evaluated from the colour silver made on a touchstone. The searches were at their height in

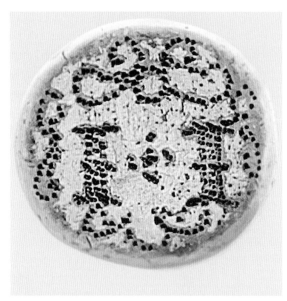

Central spoon in group of three illustrated, initials on top of seal. Diameter of seal top 9/16". Photograph by Peter Marsh

the 1630s, when there were three covering the West Country. An earlier one, not precisely dated, shows that even leading citizen John Ivie was not above a slight bending of the rules. The wardens 'did tak from one Ivy a goldsmith part of the maiors mace, and uppon assaie and trial of part thereof found it not to be 11oz 2dwts'. What followed, which was an unfulfilled threat by the wardens to break the mace, and a fine of 20 shillings, reduced to five shillings after Ivie's apologies and promises of future good behaviour, sets the tone for most future encounters between the wardens and the Salisbury silversmiths.

The 1631 search, for instance, resulted in fines on several makers, including John Greene and Robert Tyte. The one on Greene was £30, a very substantial sum for the period. Once again, it was reduced to £15 after due repentance. That search also throws up a particularly interesting name, that of George Batter, a working silversmith who never made it into the upper echelons of Salisbury society. When he died in 1664 his household goods were worth £7 12s, a long way from what Greene must have had to incur a fine of £30. Batter was living in 'Green Craft Street', with his workshop attached to his house, one of the few pieces of information about the locations of Salisbury silversmiths. There seems to be no evidence, for instance, that Ivie ever lived in Mayor Ivie House in Ivy Street, though the street name may have derived from his family. Silver Street must originally have had some connection with the trade, but nothing suggests that makers concentrated there later on.

Batter seems to have been a somewhat ill-disciplined character, fined in June 1635 for being drunk. His appearance in the 1631 records is quite a

Spoon by George Batter. Length 6.75". Note the dull colouring to the head of the spoon, indicative of the very high copper content. Photograph by Peter Marsh

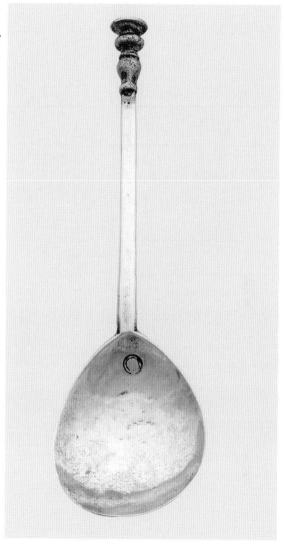

lengthy one. On being visited by the wardens and asked for examples of his work he refused, claiming to have made nothing during the previous year. This is described as 'A deluding of Mr Wardens and a resistinge of their authoritie by delayinge of their Search'. The wardens asked the mayor for assistance, as they were entitled to do, and a constable was supplied to help deal with him. Batter was escorted towards the prison, at which point he had second thoughts and sent for his wife, who brought some of his work with her. This was found to be sub-standard, and a fine of five pounds was levied. Batter of course promised not to offend again, and on account of that, and also 'Mr Wardens takeinge into consideration his povertie', the fine

Top of seal to spoon in previous illustration with initials and date 1647. Diameter of seal top 0.5". Photograph by Peter Marsh

was reduced to 11 shillings. A note in the records refers to 'George Batter, stubborn', which seems fair enough.

Two years later, the next search found Batter more co-operative, though otherwise little changed. The heads of spoons he produced for the wardens proved to have about 60% silver content rather than the statutory 92.5%, while their bodies had 80% silver. The heads were often, perhaps usually, gilded, meaning that a non–silvery look could be got away with, at least until the wardens appeared.[27]

Recently modern scientific analysis has been brought to bear on the Salisbury silversmiths. Illustrated above is a typical Salisbury spoon, with a finial of the simpler type. Its maker was almost certainly the selfsame George Batter. The mark is imperfect, but it has particular Salisbury characteristics, and resembles Batter's much more than those of other makers. The spoon's attribution to Batter by an auction house seems reasonable. It must have been a wedding present, since its top has two sets of initials, probably 'WP' and 'DP', and the date 1647.

The spoon has now been analysed by the assay office at Goldsmiths' Hall, using x–ray fluorescence spectroscopy, and the results confirm the outcomes of the searches. The bowl and stem have a silver content around 85%, while the head has the remarkable composition of 30% silver to 70% copper, bearing out suspicions aroused by a decidedly non–silvery colouration. The spoon is, in other words, about as illegal as it was possible to get without simply making some of it out of copper. To Salisbury silversmiths, particularly the less prosperous ones like George Batter, the legal standard of 92.5% silver must have been seen as a pious aspiration, which needed to be tempered by the more pressing needs of paying taxes and feeding a family.

This analysis provides absolute proof that the London wardens were fully justified in their endless campaign to bring the Salisbury silversmiths into line, and indeed they were remarkably lenient in their reduction of fines on the basis of promises not to reoffend, which they will have known were of limited worth. In 1637 a member of the Company who was travelling in the area was asked to buy some spoons from Salisbury silversmiths 'to trye

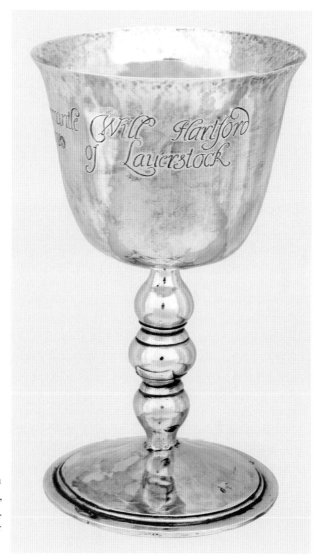

Communion cup from St Andrew's, Laverstock, dated 1697. Height 6". Photograph by Peter Marsh

if the late search had made anye reformacon amongst them'.[28] The answer, predictably, was that it had not.

Presumably the silversmiths' own local trade organisation did not worry over-much about such things. Originally there was a guild of smiths, which in the reorganisation occasioned by the city charter of 1612 became a company, with a much wider membership. This included the cutlers, a flourishing trade in Salisbury at the time, but not one with any particular link to silversmithing. The cutlers were mostly making weapons, and by the time table cutlery was produced in Salisbury to any significant extent, in the early 18th century, local silver production was effectively over, and silver handles would have been bought elsewhere. Information about training in silver making is limited, with records of formal apprenticeships tending to be for sons of Salisbury silversmiths going to work in London, but John Ivie, who was born in Wincanton, probably came to Salisbury as an apprentice under his uncle Robert Tyte. There are few glimpses of how the Salisbury workshops were organised, and there is no direct evidence as to where the silver itself came from, though the general picture is that little silver was mined in this country during the 17th century, with Spanish mines in south and central America being the probable sources for new metal, together with coins. The other key resource was old silver items, bought by the silversmiths or part-exchanged, and melted down.[29]

After the Civil War the character of silversmithing in Salisbury changed, with fewer spoons made, and different types of them appearing. There was a greater emphasis on non-spoon items, such as the two bowls, of a type known as a porringers, in Salisbury Museum, both by Thomas Hayward, one of the leading makers of this period, and one of them with a date of 1672 scratched on it.[30]

No more silversmiths became mayors, and the great days of the trade were ending. After about 1700, actual production of silver items in the city ceased, with its silversmiths now restricted either to selling on silver made elsewhere, or carrying out repairs. The three great city maces, on display in the Guildhall, were supplied by a Salisbury silversmith called Robert Wentworth, in 1749, but were actually made in London.[31]

In the final years of the 17th century city records are still referring to silversmiths (though the term used is generally goldsmith), but few items by them are known. One of the people named is Rowland West, shown as living in St Thomas's Churchyard in 1698.[32] Until recently he too was not connected to any known piece of silver, but this has changed with the discovery of a mark on a communion cup belonging to Laverstock church, the mark having been missed in the standard work on Wiltshire church

Laverstock communion cup, RW mark for Rowland West. Photograph by Peter Marsh

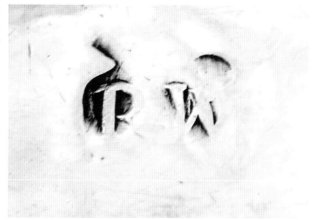

silver.[33] It consists of the initials RW, and since there is an inscribed date on the cup of 1697, and none of the other marks that would indicate a London origin, there can be little doubt that Rowland West was its maker. The cup has a baluster-shaped stem typical of its time, and nothing remains of the distinctive features of Salisbury-made cups of the previous century.

The Laverstock cup was quite possibly the final major creation of the Salisbury silversmiths, bringing to an end a story which started, in its known form at least, some 130 years before, and which has left behind it an unexpectedly rich treasury of items both religious and secular. The communion cups are still mostly in use, even if in the case of many churches they tend to be only brought out for special occasions. The spoons only surface publicly from time to time at auctions, but must number in the many hundreds if not beyond, sitting quietly in private collections. Grandly shaped and beautifully balanced, and prominently marked in their bowls, they connect us back to John Ivie and his fellows, and back to a Salisbury which it takes an effort to re-imagine, where plague lurked in the wings, and the Worshipful Company's strictures were too distant a threat to outweigh the solid commercial gain from a metal that might be, on the odd occasion, just a few pennyweight short of the mark.

## Bibliography

Baker, TH, 1910, 'The Trinity Hospital, Salisbury', *Wiltshire Archaeological and Natural History Magazine*, Vol 36, 376-412

Chandler, John, 1983, *Endless Street,* Hobnob Press

Duffy, Eamon, 1992/2005, *The Stripping of the Altars*, Yale University Press

Kent, Timothy, 1983, 'Salisbury Goldsmiths and London Wardens, 1631-1637', *Hatcher Review* 2(15), 208-217

Kent, Timothy, 1992, *West Country Silver Spoons and their Makers 1550-1750*, J.H. Bourdon-Smith Ltd

Kent, Timothy, 1993, 'Salisbury Silver and its Makers 1500 to 1700', *The Silver Society Journal Spring 1993* (all devoted to this article)

Nightingale, JE, 1889, *The Church Plate of the County of Dorset,* Bennett Brothers, Salisbury

Nightingale, JE, 1891, *The Church Plate of the County of Wilts,* Bennett Brothers, Salisbury

Oman, Charles, 1957, *English Church Plate 597-1830,* Oxford University Press

Swayne, Henry James Fowle, 1896, *Churchwardens' Accounts of S.Edmund and S.Thomas, Sarum, 1443-1702,* Bennett Brothers, Salisbury

Tim Kent's 1993 monograph is an important source of information on Salisbury silver. Kent 1983 has less information than Kent 1993, but may be easier to access. Kent 1992 has shortened versions of biographies of Salisbury makers expanded in Kent 1993, and gives much additional information on spoon making and its context.

## Notes

1. The largest display of Salisbury silver is at the British Museum, which has the Netherhampton Hoard, seven Salisbury-made spoons of early 17th century date unearthed in the village in 1907
2. Swayne, 87, 274. Kent, 1993, 6-7 quotes references to other Salisbury silversmiths from the records of the London Company of Goldsmiths in 1533 and 1536, again with no indication as to what they were making
3. Oman, 299-303
4. The Dorset examples are from Coombe Keynes and Sturminster Marshall. The latter is somewhat altered, as explained later in this piece
5. The other Wiltshire examples are from Highworth and Manningford Abbots. None of the Wiltshire chalices are currently on display
6. Oman, 111-26
7. Oman, 122
8. For an indication of the wealth of silver and other goods held by St Edmund's, see Swayne, 4-6, and Nightingale, 1891, 12-6
9. Duffy's 'Stripping of the Altars' includes a vivid account of the turbulent history of the church during this period. For the process of religious transition in Salisbury, see Cross, Claire, 'Reformation in Salisbury', *Sarum Chronicle* 13, 99-115
10. Oman 133-44
11. Baker, 408. The date comes from the Hospital accounts. The cup itself has only a maker's mark, not attributable to any specific silversmith, and where it was made is not known.
12. The Dorchester silversmith was Lawrence Stratford, examples of whose work survive at 28 Dorset churches, with at least two others known to now be in private hands
13. Kent, 1993, 13
14. Kent, 1993, 10 has lists for both counties. To the Dorset list should be added a cup from Faringdon, now a closed church
15. Kent, 1993, 13
16. As mayor, Atkins was in fact known as Thomas James (Swayne, 284). In his will he

appears as Thomas James alias Atkins (Kent, 1993, 13)

17. One of the Hampshire cups, from Vernham Dean, is on display in the treasury at Winchester Cathedral, and two of the Berkshire ones, from Childrey and Shrivenham, are in the treasury at Christ Church Cathedral in Oxford

18. Williamson, Barry, 'Relics, Rumours and Research', *Sarum Chronicle* 13, 69 has an illustration of the chapel interior (also on the back cover)

19. Nightingale 1889, 128-30 describes the chalice, without appreciating the Salisbury connection

20. See Kent, 1993, 12 for an illustration of the Sopley cup

21. Kent, 1993, passim

22. Chandler, 117 and 169-70, where Ivie's efforts to counter poverty in the city are also covered

23. Kent, 1992, 3

24. Chandler, 41-4

25. Kent, 1993, 6

26. Kent, 1993, 23-8 covers the various searches

27. Gilding was based on an amalgam of gold and mercury. Given the toxicity of the latter metal, the process may have been carried out by each silversmith for his own goods. Full-time gilding would have been a very unattractive occupation.

28. Kent, 1993, 27

29. For sources of silver see Kent, 1992, 27-33

30. Kent, 1993, 44 has a photo of a more elaborate porringer by Hayward

31. Kent, 1993, 50-1

32. Kent, 1993, 49

33. Nightingale, 1891, 32-3

J M W Turner. The Old Council House, the Market Place, Salisbury. c1800. © Cooper Gallery, Barnsley

# Fire at Wheelers, 18th September 1823

## Margaret Smith

For over two hundred years Salisbury's Council House or Guildhall has dominated the south eastern corner of the marketplace. The present building, which opened on 23rd September 1795, replaced the 14th century Bishop's Guildhall which stood on this site. The 'Turner's Wessex' 2015 exhibition at Salisbury Museum featured JMW Turner's fine watercolours of the new building and the earlier Council House, which stood near the 1922 war memorial. Turner had sketched these buildings in 1795–96, in preparation for the finished watercolours commissioned by Sir Richard Colt Hoare of Stourhead House.[1]

These exquisite watercolours provide a delightful record of Salisbury's marketplace during the Napoleonic wars and illustrate the fine appearance of the new civic building. Adjacent to the Council House in Ox Row stood the ancient timber framed premises of Messrs John and Thomas Wheeler whose business was listed as a hatter, hosier and furrier.[2] The property had recently been sold to Mr Wheeler by a Mr Cooper of Winterslow.

This building was destroyed by a disastrous fire during the evening of Thursday 18th September 1823. At the same time a grand dinner was taking place at the Black Horse Inn in Brown Street attended by a large party of city dignitaries and clergy. Amongst those present were the Bishop of Salisbury John Fisher, Rev Dr Nicholas, the Dean, Very Rev Pearson, Daniel Eyre, the Mayor of Salisbury, Viscount Folkestone, the Hon Capt Bouverie and Hon Philip Bouverie, the Rev Chancellor Marsh, Archdeacon John Fisher and William Boucher.[3]

Earlier in the day, the anniversary meeting of Salisbury Infirmary had been held, attended by the numerous Governors and Subscribers who

J M W Turner. The New Council House (or Guildhall), Salisbury. c 1805. © Cooper Gallery, Barnsley

had processed with the Mayor and members of the Corporation from the Council House to the Cathedral for the divine service. *The Salisbury and Winchester Journal* reported that Archdeacon John Fisher had preached 'a most appropriate sermon' on the subject of 'The rich and poor meet together; the Lord is the maker of them all'. A subsequent collection for the Infirmary funds amounted to £87 4s 0d.[4]

These local dignitaries were to witness the fire that engulfed Wheeler's building and threatened destruction to the surrounding area. News of the conflagration was widely reported by newspapers from London to Cornwall and Inverness.[5] It was recorded that at around 8.15pm 'the fire suddenly broke out in the rear of the extensive premises of Messrs Wheeler. . .and the flames raged with such rapidity and fury, that in the space of three hours the large shop, warerooms and adjoining dwelling house were totally destroyed'. Two pubs, the *Greyhound* which was adjoining Wheeler's was 'greatly injured and it was deemed necessary' to demolish the *Pack Horse* to prevent the spread of the fire. 'All the houses on both sides of Butcher Row were so much endangered that the inhabitants moved their goods from them as speedily as possible'.[6] The waggons of the late Mr Whitmarsh were used to move promptly the goods to safety. 'Mr Marlow's house was on fire and the warehouse of Mr Leech, spirit and gunpowder merchant, was twice on fire but was happily saved by the persons who had the direction of the fire engines or the whole of the Butcher Row would have gone'.[7] All of the constables were on duty and observed that 'a number of petty thefts were committed. No further notice was taken of the offenders apart from removing the property from their possession. The distance of the premises from the canal was so trifling that a speedy supply of water was procured but no effort could prevent the progress of the flames, the house being composed of wood'. However it was reported that 'an excellent party wall prevented the spread of the fire except for the *Pack Horse* which was promptly pulled down'.[8]

It was also reported that fortunately the calm and serene weather helped the fire fighters to bring the fire under control. The flames produced 'a vast body of ignited flakes which ascended perpendicularly into the air'. There was considerable relief expressed about the lack of wind as different conditions would have caused the fire to spread quickly to neighbouring tenements resulting in even greater destruction.[9]

News of the fire and the presence of his great friend, Archdeacon John Fisher at the scene were noted by the artist, John Constable who had returned to London a few days before, following a stay of three weeks at Gillingham vicarage with the Archdeacon and his family. His letter of 30th September 1823 requests details of his friend's involvement; 'Are you the Revd. Mr Fisher, who so nobly stemmed the fire at Salisbury?' A vivid description of the fire and his role in extinguishing the flames are given in Fisher's reply of October 2nd. He writes 'The house burnt was an old wooden one of the date of Edward III near the Council Chamber. It caught fire about 9 o'clock on a bright moon lit evening. The lathe and plaster all burnt first and then I saw the skeleton of a wooden house filled with fire. It illuminated the Market Place and made it look like a Canaletti. When the house fell, an immense black cloud of smoke rose between me and the house obscuring the object: the light breaking gloriously from the edges. The firemen all got drunk and we gentlemen turned to supply water'.[10]

The local newspaper at Windsor, the *Windsor and Eton Express*, showed a keen interest in reporting the events taking place in Salisbury, possibly as Bishop Fisher had previously served as a Canon of St George's Chapel. They reported that the Council House 'suffered more from the good intentions of the inhabitants than the flames. The stones had become very hot, there was no chance of their catching fire and as soon as the engines began to play upon the portico, the cornice began to fall to pieces and this munificent present of the Earl of Radnor has the appearance of a dilapidated building'. It appears that the Council Chamber received 'considerable injury; the pillars and the two folding doors of the Courts of Justice were very much scorched'.[11]

The press also record the valiant attempts made by the citizens to control the fire. The *Hampshire County Newspaper* reported that 'the activity of the firemen and the zeal of the inhabitants prevented the extension of the devouring calamity. Amongst the most active persons employing themselves on this lamentable occasion were the resident gentry and most of the clergy'. The *Bristol Mirror* noted that 'Mr Cove of Milford, was half drowned in water during the fire, the Rev Drs Nicholas and Davies and Daniel Eyre worked at the engines like common men and it was observed that Rev Fisher was handing the buckets'. The *Royal Cornwall Gazette* praised the inhabitants for their exertions in extinguishing the flames. 'Hundreds of persons in the more respectable ranks of life were seen working at the fire engines and hauling buckets of water with labouring men. In addition to the city engines, three arrived from Wilton which were much utilised'.[12] Nearly a week later, it was reported that the fire was 'not quite extinguished'.[13] The Mayor and Justices expressed their grateful thanks to the citizens 'for their great exertions and assistance at the calamitous fire' and also wished to thank the residents of Wilton for their' prompt, able and valuable assistance and the use of their fire engines'.[14]

The cause of the fire was unknown but a considerable portion of the goods from Messrs Wheeler's shop was saved. However all of the goods in the warerooms and almost all of household furniture were consumed. It was thought that the stock in trade and furniture were partly insured by the Sun Fire Office whose agent, Mr Cooper, visited the premises to assess the insurance claim.[15] On 6 October it reported that 'Mr Wheeler had received the full amount of the insurance on the stock destroyed by the destructive fire'. The Sun Fire Office, also the insurers for the *Pack Horse Inn*, which was demolished to prevent the further extension of the fire,' paid to Mr Endy, the full amount of the estimate of the damage done to the Pack-Horse Inn'. Other payments were made by the Old Bath Fire Office to Mr Elderton (auctioneer of Butcher Row) and Mr Casey for the full extent of their losses with all expenses. Mr Elderton publicly thanked 'his friends for removing his property from his premises and protecting his family during the alarming crisis'.[16]

Messrs Wheelers also thanked their friends for the prompt and kind assistance that they received. The business re-opened on Monday 29th September at their warehouse in Silver Street. They also requested that any property which had been 'considerately taken for protection' from the scene of the fire should be returned.[17]

By the end of October, the site of the Wheeler's building had been purchased by 'some members of Salisbury Corporation who intend to present it to the city, in order to render the Council House more conspicuous and to afford a greater facility to those who have business in the Courts'. An indenture of 1 May 1824 confirmed that Thomas Wheeler had agreed the sale of the corner tenement and premises, which had lately been destroyed by fire, to the Mayor and Commonalty of the City for £500.00.[18]

Fires were a common occurrence in urban areas where medieval buildings existed. Details of major fires are included in early 19th century newspapers across the country reflecting the interest of the general population in where these fires occurred and also reassurance that insurance claims were being fully paid by the Fire Offices.

## Notes

1   Warrall, Ian, 2015, *Turner's Wessex, Architecture and Ambition*. Salisbury Museum
2   *Early Trade Directories of Wiltshire*, 1992, Wiltshire Record Society Volume 47
3   *Salisbury & Winchester Journal* (hereafter *SJ*) 22 September 1823. *Bath Chronicle & Weekly Gazette* 25 September 1823.
4   *SJ* 22 September 1823. *Bath Chronicle & Weekly Gazette* 25 September 1823.
5   *Morning Post* 26 September 1823, *Inverness Courier* 2 October 1823, *Royal Cornwall Gazette* 27 September 1823
6   *Devizes & Wiltshire Gazette* 25 September 1823. *Bath Chronicle & Weekly Gazette* 25 September 1823
7   *Hampshire County Newspaper & South & West of England Pilot* 22 September 1823, *Devizes & Wiltshire Gazette* 25 September 1823
8   *Bristol Mirror* 27 September 1823. *Devizes & Wiltshire Gazette* 25 September 1823
9   *SJ* 22 September 1823 *Devizes & Wiltshire Gazette* 25 September 1823
10  Beckett R B (ed), 1968, *John Constable's Correspondence*. Vol 6 The Fishers. Suffolk Records Society
11  *Windsor and Eton Gazette* 27 September 1823, *Bristol Mirror* 27 September 1823
12  *Hampshire County Newspaper & South & West of England Pilot* 22 September 1823, *Bristol Mirror* 27 September 1823, *Royal Cornwall Gazette* 27 September 1823
13  *Devizes & Wiltshire Gazette* 25 September 1823
14  *SJ* 22 September 1823
15  *SJ* 22 September 1823
16  *Bath Chronicle & Weekly Gazette* 9 October 1823. *Salisbury & Winchester Journal* 6 & 13 October 1823. *Early Trade Directories of Wiltshire*. Wiltshire Record Society 1992.
17  *SJ* 22 September 1823
18  *Devizes & Wiltshire Gazette* 30 October 1823. WSHC 906/SAL/78 Indenture 1 May 1824

# Lady in a green dress

The *Sarum Chronicle* editorial team would like to apologise for the omission of the following passage from the article about Jasper Grant in last year's issue. The comments come from Rosemary Harden from the Fashion Museum, Bath:

Your rather masculine looking lady: I think that she is spot on for the 1833 date and I have to say that Chev J O C Grant was rather a good observer of dress. True she seems to have lost her left forearm, but the details of the dress from the way that the pleats fall on the bodice to the curls in the hairstyle are nicely observed.

The sitter wears what is likely to be an evening dress (both because of the low wide style of the neckline and because of the sheen effect of

the dress which suggests that the fabric is silk, a plain darker-coloured silk). The bodice of the dress is pleated either side of the centre front, with the pleats running diagonally to converge at a point at the centre front of what appears to be a separate belt with a central buckle, all of which emphasize a slender waist. The skirt of the dress (the bodice and skirt would have been all-in-one at this date) looks like it was pleated on to the waistband, probably with a technique called cartridge pleating (which looks just like a row of cartridges) at this date.

The major feature of the dress is the huge gigot sleeves, which were likely to be padded to give that enormous puffed effect.

In terms of jewellery, she is wearing a long double string of small coloured beads, which is looped at the waist, a popular fashion at this date. The brooch too, worn at the central point of the bodice, was fashionable. I'm surprised she isn't wearing dangling ear-rings, and that velvet choker seems a little unusual for this date. I've been looking at a couple of illustrations, and generally the neck is bare, almost as if an uncluttered swan-like neck was the look to go for.

Her hairstyle is great. She has sausage-shaped side curls and a top-knot, which was known as an Apollo knot, with a tortoiseshell comb behind.

Since publication of *Sarum Chronicle* 14 (2014) Jasper Grant's watercolour portrait of a lady (illustrated page 42 and here) has been acquired by the authors, David Algar and Peter Saunders, from a private collection in Canada and they have donated it to Salisbury Museum (SBYWM: 2015.6). By coincidence the passage of text accidentally omitted from the article, and quoted above, relates to the dress of the lady in this portrait.

# Author Biographies

**Dr Lucille H Campey** is a historian and author of ten books on British emigration to Canada. She is also the newsletter editor of the Dinton Historical Society.

**John Chandler** is currently Gloucestershire editor of the Victoria County History, but has researched and published extensively on the history of places in Wiltshire and Dorset, especially the Salisbury area. He was formerly general editor of the Wiltshire Record Society and joint editor of *Wiltshire Studies.*

**Alan Crosby** has been the editor of *The Local Historian* since 2001. Nationally known as a regional local historian, he has also taught extensively on many aspects of political, social and landscape history (focusing especially on the medieval and early modern periods) for universities including Oxford, Cambridge and Liverpool. His paper on the meaning of the place name Harnham was published in Sarum Studies 4 (*Harnham Historical Miscellany*) and he has recently completed an edition of some late medieval correspondence relating to a soldier serving in the retinue of the first Earl of Derby.

**Sam Cutler** is a veterinary surgeon who qualified with her husband in veterinary surgery at Bristol University before joining Endell Veterinary Group in Salisbury. When handwritten notes about the origins of EVG were uncovered during renovations, they piqued her interest. Having been involved in tracing her family history for many years, the notes formed the basis of her 'veterinary family history' research.

**Richard Deane** studied Chinese at Oxford and Leeds universities, worked in the building trade and eventually trained as a stonemason at Salisbury

Cathedral. In the mid–1990s he set up his own stonemasonry business and is now retired. He wrote the text of the primarily photographic book *Salisbury in Detail*, published by the Salisbury Civic Society in 2009.

**Steven Hobbs**, an archivist with Wiltshire Council for over 20 years, is general editor of the Wiltshire Record Society, for which he has edited volumes on glebe terriers and gleanings from parish registers.

**Sue Johnson** is a local historian with a particular interest in early Victorian Salisbury. She has been researching Edwin Young and the Art Gallery since reading a newspaper article in 1994.

**David Richards** is a retired dental surgeon who is now a Blue Badge Guide with a particular interest in the history of the people and buildings of the Salisbury area.

**Caroline Rippier** has had a keen interest in France and French culture for many years. After leaving school she studied French and also learned shorthand and typing before embarking on a working life that led to journalism which she enjoyed for more than 25 years. She has travelled widely and lived in Europe and Australia, none of which equipped her to take on chairmanship of the Salisbury Saintes Twinning Association in 2007.

**Penelope Rundle** is a retired archivist who spent nearly all her working life in the Wiltshire Record Office, at that time in Trowbridge. She was among the first Church of England women to be ordained priest in 1994, and now enjoys living in the College of Matrons in Salisbury Cathedral Close.

**Margaret Smith** is a teacher and Blue Badge Guide with a special interest in the history of Georgian and Regency Salisbury.

**Tim Tatton-Brown** is a freelance archaeologist and architectural historian, with a particular interest in ecclesiastical buildings. He is consultant archaeologist to St George's Chapel, Windsor and to Westminster School and Lambeth Palace.

**Jamie Wright** is an archaeologist working principally in southern Britain. He is now retired and lives in Salisbury.

# Index to volumes 11-15

Compiled by Andrew Minting